D0930423

The Labyrinthine Ways of Graham Greene

The Labyrinthine Ways of Graham Greene

by FRANCIS L. KUNKEL

Revised

Expanded Edition

PAUL P. APPEL, *Publisher*

MAMARONECK, N.Y.

1973

First Printing 1960
Reprinted 1973

Library of Congress Catalog Card #73-75125
ISBN #911858 — 25-3

TO LORETTA

Preface to the First Edition

THIS BOOK attempts to establish the place of Graham Greene (1904-), British novelist, playwright, essayist, and critic, in contemporary literature. There have been a few excellent articles on particular aspects of Greene's work, but book-length studies have generally relied heavily upon unsupported generalizations and analysis without comparison. I have attempted, therefore, in this present study, to see his works in their setting and to compare Greene with others in his traditions and tendencies.

Proceeding from a particular point of view as it does, my contribution is not a mere survey of Greene's writing, however. Of all the elements that comprise Greene's art, I am mainly interested in his themes and ideas, his ethical and theological preoccupations; but, most of all, I am interested in his characters and the way in which they respond to moral crises. I have chosen to emphasize these matters, because Greene's characters and themes are the most important aspect of his work as well as the most misunderstood.

In reviewing Greene's travel books and collected essays, I was so struck by his preoccupation with evil—he insists on it continually in these works—that I have organized Chapter 1 around it. The remaining chapters are likewise organized largely by various topics or themes. Preferring to deal with Greene's underlying ideas, I have tried for the most part to avoid a book-by-book survey as well as a chronological and biographical approach. I think it less mechanical and more effective to subordinate these matters to the topics and themes. For example, instead of dealing exhaustively with the influence of Henry James on Greene in Chapter 1, I treat only that aspect of James' influence, James' sense of evil, that is pertinent to my thesis at that moment. It seems sensible to defer consideration of Jamesian influence on plot construction until that is my topic—which is the case in Chapter 3. Again, rather than present a brief summary of Greene's life in the first chapter, I have discussed details of his life only when they are relevant to his fiction. Thus, the biographical items are widely scattered.

Grateful acknowledgment is made to The Viking Press, Inc., New York, and to William Heinemann, Ltd., London, for permission to quote from Graham Greene's published works. The books of Greene which are discussed in this study, with very few exceptions, have remained in print and are still available.

I wish to acknowledge a heavy debt of gratitude to William York Tindall for his encouragement, patience, and guidance throughout the writing of this book. I am also indebted to Professor Robert Gorham Davis and Philip Scharper for their helpful suggestions. Most of all, I am indebted to my wife, whose help at every stage in the preparation of this book was invaluable.

F.L.K.

Preface to the Revised Expanded Edition

SINCE THIS book was first published in 1960, Graham Greene has composed three novels, two plays, two volumes of short stories, a journal, and an autobiography. So there is obviously a need to bring the first edition up to date. The overall scheme which guided the preparation of the first edition has been retained in this expanded revision, but the principle of organization has been modified, with some necessary concession to chronology, largely in the new chapter.

To some extent, all the chapters are rewritten. At least minor changes have been made in each one. The first chapter, a description and appraisal of Greene's non-fiction, is strengthened by adding an analysis of his recent autobiography. Only minor revision has been required on the second, third, and fourth chapters devoted to the early novels, the entertainments, and the Catholic novels. The fifth has been extensively revised, to accommodate the two additional plays. A new chapter, the sixth, has been added: to deal with the three latest novels and the journal, a blueprint for one of them. The bibliography has been brought up to date, and an index is now included.

In the original study, I did not discuss all the short stories, preferring to discuss just some of the more important ones in connection with the longer works when appropriate thereto. Inasmuch as Greene's short fiction remains the least distinguished aspect of his work — a mere byproduct of his career as a novelist — I see no reason to do differently this time. Hence comments on selected short stories are scattered throughout the book.

In this edition, I have striven not only to comment on the entire Greene canon — with the aforementioned exception of the least significant short stories — but to re-evaluate thoroughly his whole achievement in the light of the radical change that has come over his work in the past fifteen or so years.

F.L.K.

St. John's University
New York
January 1, 1973

Contents

The Labyrinthine Ways
of Graham Greene

1 Travel Books and Collected Essays

GRAHAM GREENE is a voyager within as well as a voyager without. His two travel books, *Journey Without Maps* (1936) and *Another Mexico* (1939),[1] take the reader on both a physical journey and a psychical journey. But Greene is primarily the explorer of interior geography. He travels to discover himself, to make maps of his own dark interior. His travel books are voyages toward self-awareness. In them, the reader encounters a man on a quest: a modern Telemachus in search of his father. In *Journey Without Maps*, Greene relates how he went to West Africa in 1935 on the chance of finding "King Solomon's Mines, the 'heart of darkness' . . . or more simply . . . one's place in time, based on a knowledge not only of one's present but of the past from which one has emerged."[2]

Journey Without Maps and *Another Mexico* inspired two novels. *The Power and the Glory* is based on the Mexican travel book; *The Heart of the Matter*, to a lesser extent, on

---

[1] A third volume, *In Search of a Character* (1962), is sometimes classified as a travel book also. But since it is actually a meager journal of less than 100 pages and not a fully developed travel book, I shall refer to it in connection with *A Burnt-Out Case* for which it was the raw material.

[2] *Journey Without Maps*, Uniform ed. (London, 1950), p. 8. This is the first of several allusions to H. Rider Haggard and Joseph Conrad. The influence of Conrad on Greene will be treated in a later chapter.

the African travel book. Greene cannot rest from travel. He
travels incessantly in England and out of England en route
to Ireland, Scotland, France, Monaco, Italy, Austria, Poland,
Yugoslavia, Sweden, the Canary Islands, Africa, Indochina,
Malaya, Mexico, Cuba, and the United States. Like Tennyson's
Ulysses, he finds it dull to pause, "to make an end,/To rust
unburnished, not to shine in use!" Only the African and
Mexican trips culminated in travel books. In other instances—
Orient Express,[3] *The Shipwrecked*,[4] *The Third Man, Loser
Takes All, The Quiet American, Our Man in Havana*—for-
eign color, settings, and intrigue were transferred directly into
his fiction.

Never sedentary, not content to remain long in his London
flat, Greene prefers to be outward bound: to search for inspiration and subject matter or just to get away. Many excellent
contemporary works have grown out of new adventures in
distant places. A visit to India produced *A Passage to India*.
Travels in the Congo occasioned *Heart of Darkness*. A stay
among the simple fisher-folk of the Aran Islands resulted in
Riders to the Sea. Deep-sea fishing excursions off Cuba occasioned *The Old Man and the Sea*. A trip to Mexico resulted
in *The Plumed Serpent*. This contemporary interest in remote
and exotic places is a carryover from the romantic and post-
romantic movement when many artists and writers, like
Chateaubriand, Rimbaud, Gauguin, and Loti, felt compelled
to commune with earth's primitives. They fled to North
America, Africa, Tahiti, or Brittany to find an antidote to that
norm, moral and literary, against which they had always rebelled in Paris. As far as possible from the scene of early
sorrow and disorder, they sought perspective.

[3] The English title is *Stamboul Train*.
[4] The English title is *England Made Me*.

The etched economy, "ack-ack" precision, and satin texture of Greene's travel writing is belied at first by the casual charm and seemingly effortless ease. Few other writers can summon up persons and places so well so quickly. In *Journey Without Maps*, he recalls how he watched "the native women [of Freetown] rolling home magnificently from church on a Sunday morning, the cheap European cottons, the deep coral or green flounces, the wide straw hats, dignified by the native bearing, the lovely roll of the thighs, the swing of the great shoulders." In a comparably brief space, he also evokes the atmosphere of Freetown itself. "I begin to remember mainly the sunsets when all the laterite paths turned suddenly for a few minutes the colour of a rose, the old slavers' fort with the cannon lying in the grass, the abandoned railway track with the chickens pecking in and out of the little empty rotting station, the taste of the first pink gin at six o'clock."

Both travel books are digressive and subjective; both expertly interweave personal experiences and recollections of things past with superb character sketches and descriptions of place. But there are differences, too. *Journey Without Maps* is a loosely-connected series of impressions, with symbolical overtones, of Sierra Leone and Liberia, resembling D. H. Lawrence's *Mornings in Mexico*. *Another Mexico* is more autobiographical and is more clearly a blueprint for a novel.

Non-literary men find it costly to exorcize their neuroses; some authors find it profitable to exploit their obsessional compulsions. Graham Greene is one of those who find it useful to have "a private vision," because it lends "symmetry of . . . thought" and "the importance of a system"[5] to a whole shelf of books. There are two sentences by Greene, in a probing study of Walter De La Mare's short stories,

[5] *The Lost Childhood* (New York, 1952), p. 21.

that perfectly express his opinion on this subject: "Every creative writer worth our consideration, every writer who can be called in the wide eighteenth-century use of the term a poet, is a victim: a man given over to an obsession. Was it not the obsessive fear of treachery which dictated . . . James's plots . . . and was it not another obsession, a terrible pity for human beings, which drove Hardy to write novels that are like desperate acts of rebellion in a lost cause?"[6] The examples of James and Hardy suggest that an author's obsession may be detected best in the symbols he uses. Many of Greene's obsessive symbols are to be found in long autobiographical passages in his travel books.

In 1935, after landing at Freetown, capital of Sierra Leone, Greene took the train up to Pendembu. From there he crossed the frontier into Liberia and hiked down to Grand Bassa on the coast. Among the Liberians, he discovered superstitious beliefs that were remarkably like his own earliest dreams:

It is the earliest dream that I can remember, earlier than the witch at the corner of the nursery passage, this dream of something outside that has got to come in. The witch, like the masked dancers, has form, but this is simply power, a force exerted on a door, an influence that drifted after me upstairs and pressed against windows.

Later the presence took many odd forms: a troop of black-skinned girls who carried poison flowers which it was death to touch; an old Arab; a half-caste; armed men with shaven heads and narrow eyes and the appearance of Thibetans out of a travel book; a Chinese detective.

You couldn't call these things evil, as Peter Quint in *The Turn of the Screw* was evil, with his carroty hair and his white face of damnation. That story of James's belongs to the Christian, the orthodox imagination. Mine were devils only in the African sense

[6] *Ibid.*, p. 79.

of beings who controlled power. They were not even always
terrifying. . . .[7]

It was only many years later that Evil came into my dreams:
the man with gold teeth and rubber surgical gloves; the old woman
with ringworm; the man with his throat cut dragging himself
across the carpet to the bed.[8]

From these quotations it is clear that for Greene the awareness of "power"—threatening but amoral—preceded the consciousness of evil. This sense of power first evolved into the
notion of evil when Greene was a schoolboy. He attended
Berkhamsted public school, outside of London, where his
father was headmaster. Greene hated the school, with its
ugly brick buildings, its jangling bells, the all-pervasive smell
of ink. He hated weekday classes; he loved weekend freedom.
In *Another Mexico*, he recalls the prejudices of a thirteen-
year-old boy:

One was an inhabitant of both countries: on Saturday and Sunday afternoons of one side of the baize door, the rest of the week
of the other. How can life on a border be other than restless? You
are pulled by different ties of hate and love. For hate is quite as
powerful a tie: it demands allegiance. In the land of the skyscrapers, of stone stairs and cracked bells ringing early, one was
aware of fear and hate, a kind of lawlessness—appalling cruelties
could be practised without a second thought; one met for the
first time characters, adult and adolescent, who bore about them
the genuine quality of evil.[9]

He described himself as an inhabitant of two countries,
lying side by side, where "you had to step carefully: the

[7] *Journey Without Maps*, p. 219.
[8] *Ibid.*, p. 220.
[9] New York, 1939, p. 2.

border was close beside your gravel path."[10] And Graham Greene has remained faithful to this vision of man as an inhabitant of two countries; of life as something lived—restlessly and in peril—on the border between love and hate, good and evil, heaven and hell. But it was only hell that lay about him in his infancy:

And so faith came to one—shapelessly, without dogma, a presence above a croquet lawn, something associated with violence, cruelty, evil across the way. One began to believe in heaven because one believed in hell, but for a long while it was only hell one could picture with a certain intimacy—the pitchpine partitions in dormitories where everybody was never quiet at the same time; lavatories without locks: "There, by reason of the great number of the damned, the prisoners are heaped together in their awful prison . . ."; walks in pairs up the suburban roads; no solitude anywhere, at any time.[11]

For a long time his residence in hell seemed the more real, because the most intimate symbol for heaven supplied by the Anglican school chapel was "only a big brass eagle." It was not until his conversion to Catholicism in the winter of 1926 that he "began slowly, painfully, reluctantly, to populate heaven. The Mother of God took the place of the brass eagle: one began to have a dim conception of the appalling mysteries of love moving through a ravaged world—the Curé d'Ars admitting to his mind all the impurity of a province, Péguy challenging God in the cause of the damned." Despite this change, Greene could not help feeling that modern civilized life "remained something one associated with misery, violence, evil. . . ."[12]

[10] *Ibid.*, p. 1.
[11] *Ibid.*, p. 3.
[12] *Ibid.*

In the primitive Liberian hinterland, Greene discovered a simplicity that was in strong contrast with the neurotic "misery, violence, evil" of the modern civilized world. Life, less tidy and less beautiful "in the forests of the night" than in the land of skyscrapers, was somehow closer to "the heart of the matter":

I never wearied of the villages in which I spent the night: the sense of a small courageous community barely existing above the desert of trees, hemmed in by a sun too fierce to work under and a darkness filled with evil spirits—love was an arm around the neck, a cramped embrace in the smoke, wealth a little pile of palm-nuts, old age sores and leprosy, religion a few stones in the centre of the village where the dead chiefs lay, a grove of trees where the rice birds, like yellow and green canaries, built their nests, a man in a mask with raffia skirts dancing at burials. This never varied, only their kindness to strangers, the extent of their poverty and the immediacy of their terrors. Their laughter and their happiness seemed the most courageous things in nature. Love, it has been said, was invented in Europe by the troubadours, but it existed here without the trappings of civilization. They were tender towards their children (I seldom heard a crying child, unless at the sight of a white face, and never saw one beaten), they were tender towards each other in a gentle, muffled way; they didn't scream or "rag"; they never revealed the rasped nerves of the European poor in shrill speech or sudden blows.[13]

Despite "the dirt, the disease, the barbarity and the familiarity of Africa," Greene, like Rimbaud and Conrad before him, "knew the nature of the fascination which worked on" him in this primitive place. It was "the need . . . to go back and begin again."[14] He felt the need to try to remake himself by a return to the state of lost innocence. On one level,

[13] *Journey Without Maps*, pp. 86-87.
[14] *Ibid.*, p. 311.

Journey Without Maps is the record of a safari into the interior of Africa; on a deeper level, it is a safari, revealing and terrifying, into the interior of Graham Greene:

> This journey, if it had done nothing else, had reinforced a sense of disappointment with what man had made out of the primitive, what he had made out of childhood. Oh, one wanted to protest, one doesn't believe, of course, in "the visionary gleam," in the trailing glory, but there was something in that early terror and the bareness of one's needs, a harp strumming behind a hut, a witch on the nursery landing, a handful of kola nuts, a masked dancer, the poisoned flowers. The sense of taste was finer, the sense of pleasure keener, the sense of terror deeper and purer.[15]
>
> It isn't that one wants to stay in Africa: I have no yearning for a mindless sensuality, even if it were to be found there: it is only that when one has appreciated such a beginning, its terror as well as its placidity, the power as well as the gentleness, the pity for what we have done with ourselves is driven more forcibly home.[16]

G. K. Chesterton assumed that the riddle of the universe centered upon the problem of good, not evil. His books breathe incense. A faint smell of sulphur tinctures Greene's volumes. After his African journey, his favorite subject of evil becomes such an abiding presence that he is unable to put it by. It becomes his soul's "earthly freight / . . . Heavy as frost, and deep almost as life!" The cloven hoof leaves an indelible imprint on his psyche just as it has on those of Byron, Hugo, Poe, Baudelaire, Dostoyevsky, Bloy, Bernanos, Mauriac, C. S. Lewis, and Charles Williams. He experiences the vastness of evil everywhere: in his glands, in the marrow of his bones. It scratches at his nerves and raises goose pimples. It shackles

[15] *Ibid.*, p. 278.
[16] *Ibid.*, p. 312.

his characters with "adamantine chains" and scorches them with "penal fire."

II

Poets and novelists who feel the need to justify their poems and novels often become literary critics. This enables them to preach what they practice. They usually theorize on those authors or trends which played a decisive role in their own artistic development. Those to whom they played the sedulous ape, they laud; those they rebelled against, they deplore. T. S. Eliot, for instance, recognizes Dante; they are members in good standing of the same club. Eliot snubs Shelley, remiss in the payment of membership dues.

The Lost Childhood and Other Essays (1951) [16a] consists of forty-four brief essays written between the early 1930's and 1951. Seven are personal and reminiscent. Literary studies and book reviews—the kind in which the critic discusses the writer or the subject of the book without describing to any extent the book itself—comprise the remainder of this volume. Graham Greene's forays into criticism are brilliant, penetrating, literate, controversial, and partisan: partisan in the sense that he is highly partial to those authors—Henry James, Charles Dickens, Marjorie Bowen, John Buchan, and Conan Doyle—whose work is illuminated by a preoccupation with evil similar to his own. In this, his only book of literary criticism, he implies that what he learned from the adventure tales of Buchan—"how thin is the protection of civilization"—and Doyle—how to make vivid the sense of horror which hangs over familiar places—is less significant than what he learned from the novels of the other three.

In "The Lost Childhood," the essay that lends its title to

[16a]When this was reprinted in 1969, the title was changed to *Collected Essays*.

the book, Greene confesses that "the future for better or worse really struck" when, at the age of fourteen, he read Marjorie Bowen's *The Viper of Milan*. "It was," says Greene, "as if I had been supplied once and for all with a subject." "Why?" he asks, and gives his answer:

On the surface *The Viper of Milan* is only the story of a war between Gian Galeazzo Visconti, Duke of Milan, and Mastino della Scala, Duke of Verona, told with zest and cunning and an amazing pictorial sense. Why did it creep in and colour and explain the terrible living world of the stone stairs and the never quiet dormitory? It was no good in that real world to dream that one would ever be a Sir Henry Curtis, but della Scala who at last turned from an honesty that never paid and betrayed his friends and died dishonoured and a failure even at treachery—it was easier for a child to escape behind his mask. As for Visconti, with his beauty, his patience and his genius for evil, I had watched him pass by many a time in his black Sunday suit smelling of mothballs. His name was Carter. He exercised terror from a distance like a snowcloud over the young fields. Goodness has only once found a perfect incarnation in a human body and never will again, but evil can always find a home there. Human nature is not black and white but black and grey. I read all that in *The Viper of Milan* and I looked round and I saw that it was so.

Greene claims that this melodramatic yarn revealed to him the pattern of life. This pattern of "perfect evil walking the world where perfect good can never walk again" was later confirmed by religion.

There are five essays on Henry James in this collection which deserve the most judicious consideration from all commentators. That these critiques will get this judicious consideration is doubtful: orthodox Jamesians, for example, are not likely to cherish the assertion that James was fascinated by the Catholic Church. Greene is also convinced that James was driven to write by a ruling fantasy, "a sense of evil religious in its intensity." His imagination, clouded by the Pit, "attached itself to the family sense of supernatural evil and produced his great gallery of the damned": Peter Quint and Miss Jessel, Merton Densher and Kate Croy, Gilbert Osmond and Mme Merle, the Prince and Charlotte Stant, Bloodgood, and Mme de Vionnet. Convinced that James' corrupted characters are "the vehicles for a sense of evil unsurpassed by the theological novelists of our day, M. Mauriac or M. Bernanos," Greene follows him in drawing figures of men and women who breathe the very air of hell: Pinkie, Blacker, Mrs. Baines, Willi Hilfe, Harry Lime, and the half-caste.

Greene points out that the sense of evil in James' novels is always attached to the idea of betrayal by an intimate. In each instance, it is a friend who betrays Monteith, Gray, Milly Theale, Maggie Verver, and Isabel Archer. Part of Greene's fascination with *The Viper of Milan*, as we saw, stemmed from the fact that one of the central characters betrayed his friends. This kind of treachery has so appealed to Greene's imagination that he has made it one of his most persistent themes. In *The Man Within*, a smuggler informs on his best friend and his fellow smugglers. Jim Drover, under sentence of death in *It's a Battlefield*, is let down by his wife and his brother. In *This Gun for Hire*,[17] everyone—his employers, fellow underworld characters, a sympathetic girl he meets, even his own parents—double-crosses the harelipped assassin. There is concern with wartime traitors, who masquerade as benefactors, in *The Ministry of Fear*. Fowler, a British correspondent in Vietnam, betrays Pyle, an American who has saved his life, in *The Quiet American*. And all of the

[17] The English title is *A Gun for Sale*.

characters in these stories, at one time or another, break trust with God.

"It was only on the superficial level of plot," Greene feels, "that James was interested in the American visitor; what deeply interested him, what was indeed his ruling passion, was the idea of treachery, the Judas complex."[18] Again Greene finds James re-enforcing a belief that had conditioned Greene's own imagination from its earliest operation. The "Judas complex" seized hold of him as a boy when he discovered "Germinal," a poem by A. E.:

> In ancient shadows and twilights
>   Where childhood had strayed,
> The world's great sorrows were born
>   And its heroes were made.
> In the lost boyhood of Judas
>   Christ was betrayed.[19]

Greene leaves the reader guessing why the discovery of this poem provided him with one of those moments of crisis which affect the future, but that it affected the future there can be no doubt. All of Greene's characters repeat the Judas kiss. Raven, seeing the infant Christ in His mother's arms, thinks: there He lies "waiting the double-cross, the whips, the nails."

Reacting against the stock notion that James was "a social novelist primarily concerned with the international scene, with the impact of the Old World on the New,"[20] Greene contends that James "was a social critic only when he was not a religious one."[21] Greene accuses the Marxists and the critics of an

---

[18] *The Lost Childhood*, pp. 43-44.
[19] *Collected Poems* (New York, Macmillan, 1926).
[20] *The Lost Childhood*, p. 43.
[21] *Ibid.*, p. 28.

older generation of dwelling on marginalia when they dwell on James' social criticism:

Wealth may have been almost invariably connected with the treacheries he described, but so was passion. When he was floating on his fullest tide, "listening" as he put it, "at the chamber of the soul," the evil of capitalist society is an altogether inadequate explanation of his theme. It was not the desire for money alone which united Densher and Kate, and the author of *The Spoils of Poynton* would no more have condemned passion than the author of *The Ambassadors* would have condemned private wealth. His lot and his experience happened to lie among the great possessions, but "the black and merciless things" were no more intrinsically part of a capitalist than of a socialist system: they belonged to human nature. They amounted really to this: an egotism so complete that you could believe that something inhuman, supernatural, was working there through the poor devils it had chosen.[22]

Ironically, George Woodcock's assessment of Greene is similar to the standard Jamesian evaluation that Greene protests. All Greene's books, Woodcock concludes, show "the way in which society warps the natures of men and women and turns them to bitterness and evil. Theoretically, Greene may recognize original sin, but in his writing the evil in man is always less than the evil without, arising from the collective activities of society."[23] True, his books often develop a conflict between the individual and some segment of society —Raven and the munitions manufacturers in *This Gun for Hire*, D. and the reactionary conspiracy in *The Confidential Agent*, Rowe and the Nazi spy ring in *The Ministry of Fear*

[22] *Ibid.*, pp. 28-29.
[23] *The Writer and Politics* (London, Porcupine Press, 1948), p. 150.

—showing how the individual is turned to bitterness, hate, and revenge. But those microcosmic struggles between the individual and society are mere symptoms of the macrocosmic struggle between good and evil. Greene recognizes maladjustment in the social order, of course, and even launches a ripple of social criticism now and then, but he always uses darker and bolder strokes to paint the evil within man than the evil without. His characters have the major share of his interest, not his theme.

The evil that swells through the pages of Greene does not arise primarily "from the collective activities of society." He is not a social critic who attributes to society the major responsibility for the state of man. He is a "social critic" only in the sense that he criticizes the society which men make, not in that he criticizes society for making men what they are. In *Brighton Rock*, the final responsibility for Pinkie's self-destruction is charged, not to the slums in which he was raised, but to Pinkie's own free choice. Like James, Greene, at bottom, sees the individual, not the social organism, as the agent most responsible for evil. In *The Wings of the Dove*, for instance, the ultimate responsibility is attributed, not to the hypocritical respectability of the society in which Merton Densher moved, but to Densher himself, who lacked until too late the moral courage to disregard the false ideals of his society. The basic cause of evil, not to be sought in society, is the fact that "the human race," in the words of Cardinal Newman, "is implicated in some terrible aboriginal calamity."[24]

Henry James' "experience taught him to believe in supernatural evil, but not in supernatural good. Milly Theale is all human; her courage has not the supernatural support which

[24] These words are part of the epigraph to *Another Mexico*.

holds Kate Croy and Charlotte Stant in a strong coil. The rage of personality is all the devil's. The good and the beautiful meet betrayal with patience and forgiveness, but without sublimity, and their death is at best a guarantee of no more pain."[25] Another novelist whose experience taught him to believe the same way, according to Greene, was Charles Dickens. In Dickens' unhappy childhood, evil seemed more real than good; so the world of *Oliver Twist* is a Manichaean world, made by Satan, where "goodness wilts into philanthropy." In *Oliver Twist* there is a "nightmare fight between the darkness where the demons walk and the sunlight where ineffective goodness makes its last stand in a condemned world."[26] Dickens' good people are so inadequate that Dickens can only achieve happy endings and virtue triumphant by shameful tampering with the plot. Rose and Mr. Brownlow, those unsatisfactory shades of goodness who populate the daylight world, are no match artistically for Fagin, Monks, and Sykes, who seem to control the world after dark.[27]

To suspect Greene of being a satanical deviationist—as he accuses Dickens of being—spellbound before "the eternal and alluring taint of the Manichee, with its simple and terrible explanation of our plight, how the world was made by Satan and not by God, lulling us with the music of despair,"[28] is going too far. It is to forget that in Greene's universe the

---

[25] *The Lost Childhood*, p. 38.
[26] *Ibid.*, p. 56.
[27] At this point, I am paraphrasing Greene's point of view. Personally, I feel Greene minimizes the goodness in Dickens' characters. *Oliver Twist* suits his thesis. But what of the other novels? What of the blacksmith in *Great Expectations*, for example? Surely, he is no "unsatisfactory shade of goodness."
[28] *The Lost Childhood*, p. 57.

rage of personality is not all the devil's. Unlike Anatole France, Greene does not raise the harrowing supposition that the revolt in heaven was successful but that Satan suppressed the terrible tidings so as to profit from the confusion. To suspect Greene of being out of touch with supernatural good—as he accuses James of being—is also going too far. It is to forget the sublimity of the whisky priest's death in *The Power and the Glory* and the supernaturally supported moral courage ultimately exhibited by Sarah Miles in *The End of the Affair*.

Greene's own theological whimsey is a modification of the brimstone outlook—believing in supernatural evil to the exclusion of supernatural good—which he ascribes to Dickens and James. Greene sees evil, not as too formidable for good, but as an equal force with good. In *The Ministry of Fear*, he says, "the Devil—and God too—had always used comic people, futile people, little suburban natures and the maimed and warped to serve His purposes. When God used them you talked emptily of Nobility, and when the Devil used them Wickedness; but the material was only dull shabby human mediocrity in either case." Lugubriously intoning his mystique of gall-and-wormwood, Greene harks back to the Manichaean tradition.

The two opposite poles with respect to supernatural governance and evil are Manichaeism and Pelagianism.[29] They were heresies within the Catholic Church: the former founded by the Persian teacher Manes, in the third century; the latter by the British monk Pelagius, in the fifth century. Manichaeism is a dualistic theology. "The Manichaean dualism rests . . . on the absolute opposition of two substances . . . both un-

[29] In all this I am much indebted to *Satan*, ed. Bruno de Jésus-Marie, O.C.D. (New York, Sheed and Ward, 1952).

created and infinite, consequently co-eternal and equal, and wholly incompatible; Good and Evil, God and Matter."[30] (Matter is identical with the devil in Manichaeism.) On the crucial question of God and Satan the Manichee sees the Prince of Darkness as not a mere angel who rebelled against God nor even His adversary but the very rival of God. In attaining the status of a counter-God, Satan becomes an equal force with God.

The Pelagian, on the other hand, tries to reduce the dominion of God and Satan alike, by minimizing our dependence upon the One and our relationship with the other. Seeing man as wholly good, human nature as completely uninjured, he denies the need of redemption, the necessity for a Saviour. Pelagianism asserts that man is the author of his own salvation and that every impulse to goodness is self-inspired, largely unaided by divine grace. Since self-control is conceived as being entirely within man's natural power, concupiscence is little feared.

On the nature, influence, and origin of evil there is further disagreement. To the Manichee, evil is something positive, existing by and of itself. Since he holds that the amount of evil in the world arises purely from the nature of things, he regards evil as absolutely necessary. He is fascinated by the all-pervading evil which permeates the very substance of the universe. His Pelagian foe counters by contending that evil is something incidental to, not inherent in, the nature of man.

Since he assumes that evil comes from without, the Pelagian believes man to be naturally good but, at the same time, the lawful prey for the inhuman organization of society. If the

---

[30] *Satan*, p. 128.

Pelagian is an anarchist, he sees the individual corrupted by law; if an atheist, by religion; if a Communist, by the capitalist system; if a romanticist, by convention. He sees nothing inherent in man that would balk his aspirations and foil his dreams. So he denies the Fall of man. Far from exalting human nature, his Manichaean opponent belittles it. The Manichee believes man to be naturally bad, regarding the conception and formation of the human body as the work of the demon. He sees man's nature so throbbing with evil, so subject to original sin, that natural goodness is impossible.

Historically speaking, Manichaeism and Pelagianism are theological systems. But they survive today not as religions, to which people consciously adhere, but rather as patterns of temperament and even fundamental dispositions of the soul. The Manichee is inclined to regard the Pelagian as a superficial optimist; whereas the Manichee is a profound pessimist in the eyes of the other. In modern times, Pelagianism is the undefined "theology" of the great majority who, alert to the conflict between good and evil in the world, fail to see the same war raging on another front—within the human spirit. But the man who has peered into the abyss of himself knows that the enemy has infiltrated everywhere.

With so much by way of definition, we are now in a position to return to Greene and conclude that he is half-Manichaean. Greene is Manichaean in his tendency to regard humanity as cannon fodder in a war between heaven and hell, God and Satan, a war too balanced ever to be concluded; but he is decidedly non-Manichaean in his repeated emphasis on the bottomless plenitude of God's mercy and the ceaseless flow of His restorative grace. At least two of Greene's characters, however, are Manichaeans to the hilt. The tempter, "the thing behind the human actors," weeps out of the one good eye of Blacker in "The Hint of an Explanation" and blasphemes out of the mocking mouth of Pinkie in *Brighton Rock:* "Credo in unum Satanum."

III

Greene's most recent book, *A Sort of Life* (1971), is an autobiography concentrating on the author's life up to age twenty seven. Much of this self-portrait is familiar in substance to anyone who has read most of Greene's work. Scattered through his occasional writings are auto-biographical incidents which recur, in more elaborate form, here: his earliest recollection — sitting in a pram with a dead dog lying at his feet; the teenage experiments in suicide, culminating in Russian roulette; teenage psy-choanalysis; the alcoholic period at Oxford; a happy few years as sub-editor on the *London Times;* his conversion to Catholicism; his marriage; and his early writing career. And autobiographical themes from the same source, also in greater detail, reappear here: the misery of childhood as a Berkhamsted schoolmaster's son; the importance of childhood books, dreams, and fears; the early awareness of a relatively benign sadomasochism; the satisfaction of forgetfulness; a compulsive urge to travel to and in dangerous places in order to escape from chronic bore-dom; and the consolation of failure. Typically he ends his account at a point of early failure with the realization, that came to him after the publication and ephemeral success of his first entertainment, *Orient Express* (1932) , that he had not yet begun to master the craft of writing.

The only real surprise for faithful readers of Greene, to be found in *A Sort of Life,* is a pronounced change of heart towards Catholicism. The long love affair with the Rock of Peter, commencing with his conversion in 1926, is over. The later novels, to be sure, hint at a measure of disaffection but the end of the affair, never. However now it appears incontestable: the power and the glory are no longer the heart of the matter, for Greene. "In January 1926 I became convinced of the probable existence of something we call God, though now I dislike the word with all its anthropomorphic associations and prefer Chardin's 'Noosphere' . . . With the approach of death I care less and less about religious truth. One hasn't long to wait for revelation or darkness."[31] But then on the next page, he provides his admirers with a faint hope that he is only a burnt-out case, awaiting rehabilitation, for he adds: "Many of us abandon Confession and Communion [only] to join the Foreign Legion of the Church and fight for a city of which we are no longer full citizens."

[31]New York, 1971, p. 168.

2 The Early Novels

BY REASON of its theme, Graham Greene's first novel, *The Man Within* (1929), is very different from any of his other novels. By the time Greene wrote *It's a Battlefield* (1934), he was no longer preoccupied—at least, explicitly—with man's dual nature, the central theme of *The Man Within*.[1] *It's a Battlefield* and *The Shipwrecked* (1935) reflect his concern with the social and economic problems of that day. Communism is put under the novelist's microscope in *It's a Battlefield*. Capitalism is on the slide in *The Shipwrecked*.

The Man Within is a remarkably good first novel. Almost singular among contemporary first novels, it is not warmed-over autobiography in the manner of *The Way of All Flesh*, *Stephen Hero*, and *Look Homeward, Angel*. Save for stray autobiographical hints in the travel books and essays, Greene deferred the story of his nerves-naked adolescence until the recent *A Sort of Life*. Francis Andrews, the hero, inherited his creator's traits, to be sure, but he is not an idealized image of Greene himself. *The Man Within*

---

[1] Between *The Man Within* and *It's a Battlefield*, Greene wrote two novels, *The Name of Action* (1931) and *Rumour at Nightfall* (1932), which are almost forgotten. Considering them his poorest works, he has stipulated that they are never to be reissued. Since it is nearly impossible to come by copies of either, there is little point referring further to them.

is not a vise of revenge catching all the tiresome bourgeoisie, who, misunderstanding the author, failing to see the turbulence of his soul, made him suffer dark humiliations and disquieting indignation.

Arthur Calder-Marshall has rightly said that "few living English novelists derive more material from the daily newspaper than Graham Greene."[2] The action in Greene's novels is played out against a backdrop of current events: Marxist demonstrations in *It's a Battlefield;* the downfall of a tycoon in *The Shipwrecked;* the Brighton race-track murders in *Brighton Rock;* the Mexican church persecution in *The Power and the Glory;* World War II in *The Heart of the Matter* and *The End of the Affair;* the Indochinese war in *The Quiet American.*

The Man Within, a historical novel, is the exception to this flair for the topical subject. Filled with rum-runners and revenue officers, *The Man Within* has for its setting Sussex at the beginning of the nineteenth century. As the epigraph shows, the title is taken from Thomas Browne: "There's another man within me that's angry with me." Francis Andrews, a young man and the leading character, has a split personality. His inner person is constantly warring with his outer person. The theme of antithetical persons is mainly expressed through the contending higher and lower selves of Andrews. "He was, he knew, embarrassingly made up of two persons, the sentimental, bullying, desiring child and another more stern critic." But the divided-self motif also has extra-personal counterparts. "The flinching flesh" he inherited from his boorish father; "the prick of conscience" from his sensitive mother. His

[2] "Graham Greene," *Living Writers,* ed. Gilbert Phelps (London, Sylvan Press, 1947), p. 40.

pursuer Carlyon and his benefactor Elizabeth concretely personify warring factions of his nature. The chaste Elizabeth and the lewd Lucy represent his ambiguous attitude toward love.

After Andrews betrays his fellow smugglers to the excise men, he hides out in a Sussex cottage with a young woman, Elizabeth, his potential redeemer. When the captured smugglers are tried at Lewes, he testifies for the Crown. Nevertheless, his former companions are acquitted. Returning to Sussex, he commits suicide, because he knows the courageous "man within" cannot permanently conquer the cowardly man without.

This preoccupation with suicide is reflected in Greene's own life. Even before he was fourteen, he had made repeated attempts on his life. Once he drank some photographic developing fluid, under the impression it was poisonous. Later he drank a bottle of hay fever lotion. Another time he tried eating a "bunch" of deadly nightshade. He still remembers "the curious sensation of swimming through wool" after gulping twenty aspirin tablets before diving into the school swimming pool. At seventeen he tried Russian roulette as a cure for boredom. He slipped a bullet into a revolver, spun the chambers, then put the muzzle to his ear and pulled the trigger. "It was a gamble with six chances to one against an inquest."[3]

Andrews hated his cruel, domineering father, skipper of a rum-running ship, but loved his kind, understanding mother. His father used to beat him; his mother used to help him pick flowers, which they would press in an album. "Once my father was at home—he had been drinking, I think—and he found us. We were so busy that we didn't hear him when he called. He came and tore the leaves out of the album and crumpled

[3] *The Lost Childhood*, p. 175.

them in his fists." This family relationship—a mother and a son with identical romantic interests and almost no separate identity, totally estranged from an ignorant, bullying husband-father—calls to mind a similar triangular situation in the Morel household in *Sons and Lovers*, except that the Oedipus complex is mere background material in Greene's story.

Carlyon, who succeeded Andrews' father—after his death —as skipper of the *Good Chance*, is simultaneously Andrews' friend and foe. The two men love the same things: their hearts are caught up in vague romantic longings. Carlyon judges everything by esthetic, not by ethical standards. He trembles ecstatically at the sight of a sunset, and shoots a rapist, not because he injured the girl or broke the law, but because he took Carlyon out of the clouds and "gave him contact with a grubby earth." After the betrayal, Carlyon hunts Andrews relentlessly, because he spoiled Carlyon's cherished dreams— foolish, sentimental dreams of adventure, courage, and nobility. Andrews dreams the same dreams, but he has an "inner critic," the moral sense that Carlyon lacks. Carlyon stands for Andrews' romantic side; Elizabeth stands for Andrews' conscience. She is the voice of the "inner critic" appealing to "the man within." These two voices, the one "tipped always with the cool, pure poetry which it loved" and the other even nearer to music, "come in conflict for the mastery of his [Andrews'] movements. One was subtle, a thing of suggestions and of memories; the other, plain, clear-cut, ringing. One spoke of a dreamy escape from reality; the other was reality, deliberately sane."

In the last paragraph, Andrews prepares to kill himself for failing to protect Elizabeth, for allowing her to sacrifice her life for his safety. At this point, he learns that he can never remain wholly faithful to "the man within." He experiences "no fear of death, but a terror of life, of going on soiling himself and repenting and soiling himself again." *The Man Within* is the story of a man who faces his enemies and conquers the damaging spirit of his father but who is destroyed, and with him the only woman who ever loved him, because he cannot conquer himself.

Elizabeth is the promise of Andrews fulfilled. Beholding her in death, Andrews feels that her life "had given a meaning and a possibility to holiness and divinity." Of all Greene's characters, she remains the most saintly. The whisky priest and Sarah Miles soar as high, perhaps even higher, but they started much farther back—as far back as sin. Elizabeth's real kinsfolk are to be found outside the pages of Greene— Billy Budd, Prince Myshkin, and Strindberg's Eleanora Heyst (*Easter*). Like the seaman, Elizabeth must die because, being too good, she is a constant reproach to the evil men about her; like "the idiot" she must endure vilification without justification; and like the angelic Eleanora she has so uncanny a perception of the motives that direct people's lives that she is a source of strength to those around her.

The *real* Andrews is not a coward but "the man within." In order to become "the man within" he needs Elizabeth. She encourages him to attend the trial at Lewes and testify against the men he betrayed, to show he has more courage than they. Bolstered by Elizabeth's living presence and inspiring example, Andrews' true self is almost invincible. But in her absence at Lewes, he succumbs to his false self: he obeys "the restless prick of desire" with Lucy, a harlot. Afterwards, he is grieved by the thought of the act, considering it a sign of disloyalty to Elizabeth. It is not far-fetched to see Elizabeth and Lucy as human embodiments of Andrews' two states of being: Elizabeth his strong occasional self; Lucy his weak habitual self.

Elizabeth represents the spirit; Lucy the flesh. To the extent to which Andrews redeems himself, Elizabeth is the agent of his salvation. She "seemed to carry far behind her eyes, glimpsed only obscurely and at whiles, the promise of his two selves at one, the peace which he had discovered sometimes in music." To the extent to which Andrews destroys himself, Lucy is the agent of his damnation. "Are you a devil as well as a harlot?" he asks her.

Elizabeth and Lucy divide the female world between them so far as Andrews is concerned. He covets Lucy's body; she is lewd like his father. He yearns for Elizabeth's "deep-breasted maternal protection"; she is pure like his mother. He goes for passion exclusively with Lucy; with Elizabeth physical desire is feeble. Like Marlow, in *She Stoops to Conquer*, he has no inhibitions in the company of wenches, but in the presence of modest young women he is overwhelmed by a sense of inferiority. Andrews downgrades himself with Elizabeth, because he feels himself beneath her. He is afraid to kiss her lest her lips be defiled by the touch of his. The sexual act suits Lucy; it would degrade Elizabeth in Andrews' eyes. "I'll ask for you only when we're married and that as a favour which I don't deserve. . . . You are holy. I don't see how I can ever touch you without soiling you a little." This snobbish attitude toward sex—snobbish because it implies that sex is not good enough for some people—is associated with a puritanical attitude. Overhearing a planned assignation in Lewes, Andrews angrily curses the "damned lechers."

Graham Greene's novels may be divided into three groups: the pre-Catholic novels, *The Man Within*, *It's a Battlefield*, *The Shipwrecked*; the Catholic novels, *Brighton Rock*, *The Power and the Glory*, *The Heart of the Matter*, *The End of the Affair;* and the post-Catholic novels, *The Quiet American, A Burnt-Out Case, The Comedians, Travels with My Aunt.* The Catholic novels are alike, but different from the other two classes, in that the protagonist is a Catholic playing a dangerous game, called virtue and sin, for high stakes, called salvation and damnation. The "game" is a vocation to which the characters in the Catholic novels dedicate themselves; it is a mere avocation for a few of the characters in the early novels. *In The Man Within,* for example, there are several cryptic allusions to the life of Christ and the medieval morality play. In the latter connection, Andrews, pulled one way by the flesh and by the spirit another, is Everyman. Lucy and Elizabeth are the two sides of woman: body and soul, sweetheart and mother. Jennings, Elizabeth's guardian as a child, is the spirit of jealousy. Carlyon is pride, Luciferean pride: he stands dressed in black on a high hill and offers Andrews anything in the world.

But only infrequently does Andrews see Carlyon as the tempter. More often he sees him as a savior—on one occasion as Elizabeth's savior. "She would be safe with Carlyon. What did Carlyon's anger against him matter? He was Elizabeth's guardian now, to keep her safe from the Joes and Hakes of an embittered world." Carlyon is ugly. He has "broad shoulders, a short thick neck, a low, receding, ape-like brow," but he also has "dark eyes that in a flash tumbled to the ground the whole of the animal impression which the body had raised." Andrews thinks of him as "a Godlike and heroic ape." It is the "Godlike" quality that is paramount in many of the dealings that Andrews has with Carlyon. There is often the suggestion that Carlyon is another Christ and Andrews one of his disciples. After the betrayal Carlyon says of Andrews, "He's a sort of Judas." Andrews betrays Carlyon after spend-

ing three years with him. He contemplates going to Carlyon
as a sinner would go to Christ. "Why, indeed, should he not
go to Carlyon and confess the wrong he had done and explain?
. . . He would go as the woman who had sinned went to Christ,
and the comparison seemed to him to carry no blasphemy."

Many major obsessions and themes that haunt the
later novels may be found here in this first one: woman
competing against woman for the hero (and the reverse of
this in *The End of the Affair* and *The Quiet American*); the
dichotomy in the soul, the preoccupation with betrayal and
loyalty, the manhunt, and the "terror of life." They recur
subject to an important difference, however: in *The Man
Within* Greene does not sufficiently integrate his obsessions
with his characters, whereas in the later novels his traditional
themes are so embodied in the characters and merged with the
situation as to be inseparable from them. For instance, the
too neat division of Andrews' two selves is not nearly so convincing as is the unified presentation of soul-tearing in the
person of the whisky priest. Nor does the spectacle of Andrews
torn between two women have anything like the largeness of
life that is encountered when Scobie is confronted with a
comparable situation. Least of all are the oversimplified portraits of Lucy and Elizabeth any match for the complex portrait of Sarah Miles, who believably blends in a vital way the
two conditions of sin and virtue they separately represent in a
somewhat unbelievable way. These later characters are perfect
vehicles for Greene's obsessive themes.

Assessing literary influences is always a difficult matter,
even in a first novel. But the theme of man's two selves in *The
Man Within* obviously owes much to Dostoyevsky and Freud.
This is not to say that the young Greene necessarily read

Dostoyevsky or even Freud, but they had discovered a territory which novelists felt compelled to explore.[4]

Looking within himself, Dostoyevsky found the problem of multiple personality. Many of his characters have deranged personalities split by haunting doubts. "Do you know," says Versilov in *A Raw Youth*, "I feel as though I were split in two? . . . It's just as though one's second self were standing beside one. One is sensible and rational oneself, but the other self is impelled to do something perfectly senseless. . . ."[5] Golyadkin in *The Double* with his two strange selves, which are thrown into a continuously dramatic juxtaposition, illustrates this perfectly, if somewhat obviously. Raskolnikov in *Crime and Punishment* with his two conflicting personalities, one projected as Svidrigailov, illustrates this no less perfectly but with far greater subtlety.

But the character of Dostoyevsky's whom Andrews most resembles is Stavrogin (*The Possessed*), who has been hailed by Thomas Mann as "one of the most weirdly attractive characters in world literature."[6] Stavrogin has two extra-personal selves. Kirillov represents his ideal-making self; Pyotr Stepanovitch his ability to act. I have already shown how Elizabeth and Lucy can well stand for two sides of Andrews' character. It thus suffices merely to observe that Elizabeth, like Kirillov, is the shining vision while Lucy, like Pyotr Stepanovitch, is the shabby, inadequate realization of it.

[4] Greene does not mention Freud at all and he mentions Dostoyevsky only twice in passing. In connection with two of the aforementioned essays on Henry James, Greene refers to Dostoyevsky as obsessed with the sense of evil (*The Lost Childhood*, p. 28) and as explicitly religious (*The Lost Childhood*, p. 38).

[5] New York, Dial, 1947, p. 553.

[6] Introduction to *The Short Novels of Dostoyevsky* (New York, Dial, 1945), p. xi.

In England Robert Louis Stevenson followed the pioneering efforts of the Gothic novelists and Dickens in the field of multiple personality. Even though Greene dismisses *Dr. Jekyll and Mr. Hyde* (1886) as a product of Stevenson's immaturity,[7] *The Man Within* belongs to the same tradition—novels concerned with the nature of self.

"The Secret Sharer" (1912), brief as it is, is Joseph Conrad's boldest excursion into an ambivalent personality and is one of the finest English works in this genre. Newly appointed to his command, the young captain, who is the narrator of "The Secret Sharer," has to detach himself from his darker self. In having to exorcize the influence of his cowardly father and the influence of amoral Carlyon, Andrews is confronted with much the same problem. Looking at the murderer Leggatt, the symbol of his subconscious impulse to evil, the captain muses, "It was, in the night, as though I had been faced by my own reflection in the depths of a sombre and immense mirror."[8] The climactic scene in Elizabeth's cottage, where Andrews' courage is put to the test, is similar to the scene where the captain's self-mastery is tried. Taking his ship perilously close to shore, without going aground, to enable Leggatt to escape, he surmounts the first critical test of his navigation. The ship's danger symbolizes the abyss to which self-knowledge drives the captain. Elizabeth's danger has comparable symbolic value for Andrews. The captain emerges from the brink of disaster, the better for it; Andrews, as we have seen, teeters and loses his footing—even if he does not plunge into the crater.

Graham Greene, here as elsewhere—"Heart of Darkness" and *Lord Jim*—has an affinity with Conrad, even though

[7] *The Lost Childhood*, p. 66.
[8] *'Twixt Land and Sea* (New York, Doubleday, 1924), p. 101.

Greene is only half aware of it. He complains of the dimness of Conrad's religious sense:

Conrad was born a Catholic and ended—formally—in consecrated ground, but all he retained of Catholicism was the ironic sense of an omniscience and of the final unimportance of human life under the watching eyes. . . . Conrad's similarity is to the French, once a Catholic nation: to the author for example of *La Condition Humaine:* the rhetoric of an abandoned faith. "The natural degradation to which a man's intelligence is exposed on its way through life": "the passions of men shortsighted in good and evil": in scattered phrases you get the memories of a creed working like poetry through the agnostic prose.[9]

True, there is no explicit preoccupation with things Catholic in any of Conrad's books. "Yet," as Charles Brady observes, "his habit of imagery is often Catholic; and his great frames of moral and theological reference are ineluctably Catholic, however much the latest Conrad critics may prefer to describe these as archetypal instead."[10] Add to this Conrad's concern with fallen man as a spiritual exile and the way he endows man's suffering with significance and you are not far from Greene's belief in original sin and his faith in the potential efficacy of human suffering. To the next chapter I leave the documentation of the precise ways in which Greene is Conradian.

II

There is a multiplicity of crosses in Greene's work: the sign of the cross, the cross that every man is called upon to bear in

[9] *The Lost Childhood*, p. 99.
[10] "Conrad: A Polish Palinurus," *America*, September 21, 1957, p. 649.

life, the double-cross, and the crisscross of intrigue. The first two crosses are met with most frequently in the Catholic novels; the crisscross of intrigue in the so-called entertainments; the double-cross everywhere, but predominantly in these early novels. Andrews informed on Carlyon, the man whose very voice he thrilled to, and betrayed Elizabeth, the woman he loved more than his own life. In *It's a Battlefield*, the theme of betrayal is enlarged to include all the characters as well as the pivotal character. This novel, set in London, describes the reactions and destinies of certain people connected with a bus driver sentenced to death for murdering a policeman during a Communist party rally in Hyde Park.

The bus driver, Jim Drover, never appears on the scene directly: the reader learns about him through the thoughts, words, and deeds of the other characters. He is reminiscent of Virginia Woolf's Jacob (*Jacob's Room*, 1922), who is also an absent center, seen by the reader only as he is observed by those who come in contact with him. Jim's brother, Conrad Drover, chief clerk in an insurance office, devotes himself tirelessly to the cause of having Jim's death sentence commuted. Jim's anguished wife, Milly, turns to Conrad for help, relying on him completely. The Police Commissioner, refusing to take sides in the matter, thinks the administration of justice no part of his business. He advises the Home Secretary "that it will have no effect, whether he hangs Drover or reprieves him." Oscar Wilde's line, "each man kills the thing he loves," suits each of the major characters and the minor ones besides. Like Judas, each of them betrays the one he has reason to love most.

Like Andrews, Conrad Drover is a man alone. The two of them have brethren aplenty in Greene's early novels: homeless men pining for domesticity and an end to all strife; friendless men isolated from their co-workers, even their families, by reason of superior education, imagination, intelligence, or wealth. Conrad dramatizes his sense of isolation and his lack of love by wearing dark clothes and carrying an attaché case. His habitual solitariness stamps his old-young face with pallor and makes his tightly strung nerves twitch. He is cut off by his brains from the group to which he would ordinarily belong:

Brains had only meant that he must work harder in the elementary school and suffer more at the secondary school than those born free of them. At night he could still hear the malicious chorus telling him that he was a favourite of the masters, mocking him for the pretentious name that his parents had fastened on him, like a badge of brains since birth. Brains, like a fierce heat, had turned the world to a desert round him, and across the sands in the occasional mirage he saw the stupid crowds playing, laughing, and without thought enjoying the tenderness, the compassion, the companionship of love.

His superior intellect and his "pretentious" name have conspired to sabotage his happiness from the start. No wonder he wishes they belonged to another. He longs to be like his brother, free of them. No one takes him seriously, "as a man, as a chief clerk, as a lover," so that he envies his brother's strength and stupidity. For his brother's serene obtuseness, he would gladly exchange his brains and cleverness.

Conrad has two loves, his brother and his sister-in-law. Ironically he betrays the one and makes the other miserable. His doomed relationship with Milly expresses the theme of betrayal. His love for her recalls Andrews' love for Elizabeth: a love largely uncomplicated by lust. Before the murder, Conrad was content just to be with Milly: to open bus windows for her, to pretend "to understand the names written on the steel labels" in Kew Gardens, to sip tea quietly "in the tropical heat of the Palm House." So, after Jim's imprisonment, it is pity, rather than lust, that finally drives Conrad into Milly's bed. "If he had felt the slightest lust, he would have fled; it was the unexcitement in his love, the element of pity, that kept him there. It seemed unbearable to him that she should suffer." In this well-meaning but hopeless attempt to spare her anything he could, he foreshadows Scobie who, also moved by pity, frantically and futilely tries to shield those he loves from pain. The many betrayals in this book are coated with irony. The people whom Conrad hates—his fellow clerks, the manager, the Police Commissioner—he keeps trust with; but the brother whom he loves, he betrays.

Francis Andrews and Conrad Drover do not associate the sexual act with love. They associate the sexual act with lust or pity. Andrews and Elizabeth, Conrad and Milly shrink from "the direct contact of skin with skin." Yet Andrews has no such inhibition with Lucy, and Conrad enjoys "the thrust of lust" with prostitutes. Going to bed was simple, Conrad thought, "It was only love which complicated the act." He distinguishes sharply between love and love-making: only lust is expressed in love-making. "Before their bodies had known each other, they had been closely acquainted. . . . He could believe that she loved him in a way, and that way, though it provided no satisfaction, was better than this . . . this shared ignorance of anything beyond a touch, a sense of physical closeness, a heat and a movement." Love culminates in a platonic relationship, so far as he is concerned. Lying in bed with his brother's wife, feeling miserable and filled with guilt, Conrad reflects: "Love had been close to him, in the kitchen, before the glow and the hum of the gas, between chair and chair, which had escaped him now in the bed, in the dark." It is all a matter of furniture: a bed seems a less propitious place for love than the kitchen stove.

In the early novels, "love is expressed in talk rather than lovemaking and ends in death."[11] Andrews and Elizabeth die by their own hands, while Conrad is killed by a skidding automobile. Only Milly is spared, but perhaps for nothing more than a living death. In these same novels, lust, expressed by Andrews in passion, ends in disgust; pity, expressed by Conrad in sexual relations, ends in despair. When Lucy asks Andrews if he has enjoyed himself with her, he replies, "I've wallowed . . . You've made me feel myself dirtier." His spirit is left curiously unsatisfied; only "his dirty lusting body" is satisfied. After two lugubrious adulteries with Milly, Conrad is reduced to despair. "The act which was to have been his armour against life, the secret inner pride, 'Even I am loved,' had betrayed him, had driven him along streets too many to count. . . . Milly, too, had betrayed him; she had given him the only thing he wanted, a thing he had never had the least hope of obtaining, and it had proved: something lovely over too quickly, weeping in the night, sleeplessness, condemnation, despair." The motive for this pitiful pleasure—to push back loneliness, his own and Milly's—is not only unattained, but the sense of loneliness is even accentuated. "For he was lonely, as lonely as he had ever been in spite of his passion and what he once would have considered his success."

Goaded by this acute loneliness, Conrad gradually builds up a sense of hatred against the Police Commissioner whom he holds responsible for all his troubles. He thinks "of how a word from that man might have saved Jim; if the police evidence had been given a little more sympathetically, if they

[11] Kenneth Allott, *The Art of Graham Greene* (London, Hamish Hamilton, 1951), p. 48.

had admitted to having clubbed women, the jury would have recommended him to mercy." But the idea of personal vengeance does not occur to the cautious, conservative Conrad until after his pitiful union with Milly. Then as a result of an odd chain of reasoning he suddenly finds himself capable of murder. "When a cannibal ate his enemy, he received his enemy's qualities: courage or cunning. When you lay with your brother's wife, did you not become, receiving the same due as he received, something of the same man, so that if you were weak, you became strong; clever, you became stupid? For an instant last night he had been his brother, he became capable of killing a man." No longer frightened by the word "murderer," he tries to shoot the Police Commissioner but in the act of so doing is killed by a skidding automobile. It is ironical that the revolver Conrad uses in the attempted murder is, unknown to him, loaded with blank cartridges. It is doubly ironical that Conrad, the most careful, prudent person in the novel, should do the most careless, imprudent thing in the mistaken notion that it would benefit Jim.

The theme of *It's a Battlefield* is also presented ironically. Social justice—or what passes for it—is the theme. Justice demands that the State show mercy to the guilty husband but deny it to the innocent wife. Jim's life is spared: the death sentence is commuted to eighteen years imprisonment. "Drover wasn't afraid of death, but he is very fond of his wife," so he shows his "gratitude" by vainly trying to commit suicide. But Milly's life is not spared: she is sentenced to a living death. She is expected to do the impossible: to "be faithful for eighteen years to a man she sees once a month," the man she loves. He has fear in his cell but hope too. She has the more intense pain: "the gossip in the fish-and-chips shops, the kind neighbours, and the pain of Monday mornings with the washing for one hung out in the back garden, and the voices calling to and fro over the wooden fences."

It's a Battlefield, more than any of his other novels, contains Greene's criticism of the social order. The Police Commissioner and Caroline Bury, a wealthy, charitable widow, are alone "in not caring for their own troubles, for not fighting their own battle in ignorance of the general war." Three questions are addressed by Caroline to the Commissioner: "Do you believe in the way the country is organized? Do you believe that wages should run from thirty shillings a week to fifteen thousand a year? . . . Do you think I've the right to leave two hundred thousand pounds to anyone I like?" Caroline deplores economic injustice, but she is not spiritually myopic. She sees beyond. She relates economic injustice to a wider context—to the injustice of life itself—when she adds: "It would be maddening to die now, with the world in the state it is, if one hadn't Faith."

The Police Commissioner too has moments when he bemuses himself with the idea that one day the millennium will be achieved on earth. "He was filled, under the shadow of retirement, beneath the nausea which fogged his sight as he rose too quickly from the table, with a passionate desire for an eternal life, but an eternal life on earth, watching the world grow reasonable, watching nationalities die and economic chaos giving way to order." But the dream pales when he realizes that the future fulfillment of it, even if possible, would only usher in a new and greater injustice. "It would not be enjoyed by the most selfless. . . . It would be enjoyed arbitrarily by certain people who happened to be alive in a certain century, by adventurers and politicians and swindlers among the rest. Those who had fought hardest for it would probably be dead. That he himself would be dead was not unfair; he had not helped; he had served those who paid him; he had stood aside."

Since Caroline and the Commissioner alone are endowed with a vision broad enough to encompass the whole battlefield, it is only reasonable to regard them as spokesmen for Greene, the Greene who is a passionate seeker after social justice and yet no reformer deluding himself with utopian myths. Greene is wholly sincere in his desire to see injustice liquidated. But he knows that the problem cannot be solved by a team composed of psychiatrists and social psychologists, because Agape and Eros contain something which eludes and transcends all psychological techniques. In *Journey Without Maps*, Greene deliberately disassociates himself from these social engineers. "There are others, of course, who prefer to look a stage ahead, for whom Intourist provides cheaper tickets into a plausible future, but my journey represented a distrust of any future based on what we are." A satiric portrait of a Communist intellectual, Mr. Surrogate, in *It's a Battlefield*, attests to Greene's impatience with woolly-minded idealists. Mr. Surrogate loathes people; he loves ideas. "The lovely abstractions of Communism had lured him into the party—Comradeship, Proletariat, Ideology." But he is disappointed: "he resented Drover's intrusion as an individual to be saved and not a sacrifice to be decked for the altar." Mr. Surrogate always thinks in terms of sacrifice—other people's. "There is no cause for grief," he declares at a Communist rally. "Every faith demands its sacrifice. When Drover dies, the Communist Party in Great Britain will come of age."

The principal characters in *It's a Battlefield* have many traits in common with the principal characters in *The Man Within*. Conrad fleeing from himself and his conscience is reminiscent of Andrews. He has had a most unhappy childhood which never ceases to haunt him. He is a trapped man with a divided nature. While they share many similar traits, Conrad is the more believable character because of the way he is presented. The division in his nature is not attributed to fastidiously separated higher and lower persons, as is the case with Andrews. The subtle, ambiguous motives and actions woven around Conrad are a far more sophisticated and satisfactory mode of presentation. It is an unmistakable sign of technical and psychological growth on Greene's part when he no longer regards the counter-forces within a man as mutually exclusive.

The female characters in *It's a Battlefield* are also more convincing. Milly and her sister, Kay, are reminiscent of Elizabeth and Lucy. Milly is good and right by nature; she inspires the men around her. Kay, who "never felt more at home than in a bed or a man's arms," takes her pleasure where she finds it—and she finds it almost everywhere. "Milly felt shy before her younger sister. She stood at the edge of loneliness, carrying a little of the vacancy of empty rooms in her blue abashed eyes, while Kay brought in with her a world of men. After five years of marriage Milly felt inexperienced and stupidly innocent in front of Kay." Milly and Kay accordingly do the same thing as Elizabeth and Lucy—they suggest the antithesis between love and lust—but they do it more artistically. Milly and Kay are independent, self-contained beings; whereas Elizabeth and Lucy are, to too great an extent, merely Andrews' divided self fleshed out. As characters in and of themselves, they remain shadowy.

In respect of structure, *It's a Battlefield* is also superior to *The Man Within*. The whole complex of experience treated is so shaped as to form a novel extraordinarily taut. By comparison, *The Man Within* is loose and sprawly. The writing is brisk and the verbal excitement sustained in *It's a Battlefield*. Static stretches and an uneven style characterize the first novel. Juxtaposed thought and action make occasional portions of *The Man Within* seem static. By fusing the thought and action in a stream of consciousness, this difficulty is overcome in the later novel. As the Commissioner, for example, walks through London of a Sunday morning, his interior monologue keeps the reader informed of his thoughts and his journey simultaneously. Walking from his home through the city, the Commissioner comes upon localities and streets which carry relevant associations and dredge up memories of a long tour of duty in the East. The uneasy peace of Sunday in Pall Mall, which disturbs him like the dead peace after a jungle massacre, illustrates this.

The Man Within is a technically simple novel. Chronological order governs the sequence of events and the point of view throughout is largely Andrews'. In *It's a Battlefield*, chronological order more or less governs the sequence of events, but subject now to a point of view which switches from character to character. *It's a Battlefield* is based on twenty-five or more short scenes. These scenes are grouped into five chapters or parts. A new scene commences every time the point of view changes. This shifting from the point of view of one character to the point of view of another brings the individual characters into sharper focus than was the case in *The Man Within* and clarifies the intent of the work as a whole. In *The Man Within* when the other characters are not seen through Andrews' eyes, they are described directly by the author himself. But there is no need for this kind of explicit authorial intervention in *It's a Battlefield*, because every character is seen through the eyes of every other character. Andrews' portrait of his father is the sole version the reader gets, whereas the portraits of even the minor characters in the later novel are composite versions. A case in point is Conder, the frustrated journalist with the immature outlook on life. He lives in a fictitious world to escape the discontent and unhappiness of his real one. Conder is a bachelor who tells his fellow characters that he is a happily married man with six children. Those who know only the fictitious Conder envy him; those who know the real Conder naturally pity him.

III

The Shipwrecked is structurally similar to *It's a Battlefield*. Greene repeats his sweeping shifts in point of view and his use of the interior monologue, but with a sureness of touch that was sometimes absent in the preceding novel. *The Shipwrecked* consists of seven parts, with each part, save the last, divided into several scenes. Each scene presents the point of view of one of the major characters. There is the point of view of Eric Krogh (based on Ivar Kreuger), self-made Swedish industrialist, who is bored with his vast financial empire and derives no pleasure from his enormous wealth. There is career woman Kate Farrant's point of view. There is the point of view of her twin brother, Anthony, a ne'er-do-well, who is "unreliable, deceitful in small ways, hopeless with money." Other points of view belong to Minty, Hall, and young Andersen. Minty is a pathetic journalist who makes a meagre living reporting the doings of Krogh. Hall is Krogh's trouble-shooter, a man without a conscience. Young Andersen is a naive, stubborn employee of Krogh's.

Graham Greene makes more sophisticated use of the interior monologue in *The Shipwrecked*. Conrad's soliloquy on a Sunday walk about London, for instance, for all its frantic quality, is more logical and chronological than, say, Anthony's stream of consciousness in part one. Conrad's self-revelation is interrupted by a small boy's laughter, a woman's stare, a panhandler's request for money, shouting children, barking dogs, whispering lovers, and grinning whores. Anthony's is unbroken. Anthony's free association loops around the present and the past simultaneously. Except for a single childhood recollection, Conrad's is all rooted in the present. Both novels feature juxtaposed monologues. Conrad's monologue on a walk in London balances the Commissioner's on a similar stroll. And Anthony's unimpeded flow of feelings and thoughts in London is supplemented by Kate's in Stockholm.[12]

Imbedded in the streams of consciousness are certain recurring motifs. An illustrative case occurs in *It's a Battlefield*, where the remembrance of a lantern slide serves as a symbol of Conrad's unbearable sense of responsibility. Whenever he feels tired and depressed, his thoughts are held by the memory of a picture of starved, naked native children projected on a screen in a stove-heated schoolroom. He is as haunted by his responsibility for these black children as he is for Milly. An equally illustrative case occurs in *The Shipwrecked*, where the winning of a toy tiger as a prize at a shooting gallery serves as a symbol of Anthony's evasion of responsibility. Whenever he fells frustrated and inadequate, he likes to shoot at a fair, "the only performance at which he was supremely skilful." He finds it less painful to hit ping pong balls dancing up and down in a fountain than to get entangled in human affairs and become genuinely involved with people.

[12] In *The End of the Affair* the novelist, Maurice Bendrix, who on occasion speaks for Graham Greene, is questioned about technique. "You used the stream of consciousness in one of your books. Why did you abandon the method?" "Oh, I don't know," Bendrix replies in his supercilious way. "Why does one change a flat?"

Conrad's lantern slide and Anthony's toy tiger, like Wilder's bridge of San Luis Rey and Meredith's cherry tree, are examples of what E. K. Brown calls "fixed symbols" and E. M. Forster calls "banners."[13] But Forster and Brown prefer what the latter calls an "expanding symbol." As an example of an "expanding symbol," he cites Melville's white whale. Since Brown's account of the difference between these two methods of thematic elaboration is the best we have, I shall quote it at length:

The fixed symbol is almost entirely repetitious; the expanding symbol is repetition balanced by variation, and that variation is in progressively deepening disclosures. By the slow uneven way in which it accretes meaning from the succession of contexts in which it occurs; by the mysterious life of its own it takes on and supports; by the part of its meaning that even on the last page of the novel it appears still to withhold—the expanding symbol responds to the impulses of the novelist who is aware that he cannot give us the core of his meaning, but strains to reveal now this aspect of it, now that aspect, in a sequence of sudden flashes.[14]

The stone statue in *The Shipwrecked* is an expanding symbol. For each of the major characters the statue is not the same statue. It is given a surplus of meaning, and that meaning is never close to explicit statement. To the end of the novel it retains a fringe of unexhausted suggestion.

Irony also abounds in *The Shipwrecked*. Serving the same function in this novel as in *It's a Battlefield*, irony highlights

[13] E. M. Forster, *Aspects of the Novel* (New York, Harcourt, 1927); E. K. Brown, *Rhythm in the Novel* (Toronto, Toronto University Press, 1950). For still another cogent treatment of recurrent images, see William York Tindall, *The Literary Symbol* (New York, Columbia University Press, 1955).

[14] Brown, *op. cit.*, p. 57.

the theme of betrayal—the most important theme in these early novels. The betrayals occur here against a background of international finance. Krogh betrays himself because he lacks self-understanding. He thinks himself emancipated from the past. "He had always despised people who thought about the past. To live was to leave behind; to be as free as a ship-wrecked man who has lost everything." A green stone statue of a pregnant woman, made by Sweden's greatest sculptor, stands in the circular courtyard of Krogh's lavishly equipped ultra-modern plant. At first this statue fills him with a faint sense of regret and uneasiness, and he dislikes it. But later it delights him, when he suddenly realizes that "it wasn't the past, it wasn't something finished to the nipple, to the dimple, to the flexed knee: it was something in the present tense, some-thing working its way out of the stone." The statue at this point is an image confirming Krogh in his illusion that he has left the past behind, that he is now, at middle age, "as free as a shipwrecked man."

Eric Krogh does not realize that he is a prisoner of his own past. That is his tragedy. "Krogh, the internationalist, who had worked in factories all over America and France, who could speak English and German as well as he could speak Swedish, who had lent money to every European govern-ment," was born, amidst great poverty, in a peasant's hut be-side the shores of Lake Vätten. "The gawkiness of the poor past" makes him forever ill-at-ease in society. He values "the correctness of a machine, the correctness of a report," more than the unpredictable behaviour of a human being. "He thinks in figures, he doesn't feel vague things about people." Char-acters like Krogh and Mr. Surrogate, the Communist intellec-tual in *It's a Battlefield*, favor the abstract and the impersonal, because they find that people are more difficult to get along with than statistics. Krogh is caught by twenty years of prosperity. Money and success isolate him. He cannot even talk to his own employees without feeling uneasy. "E. K. on the ash tray; E. K. on the carpet; E. K. flashing on above the fountain . . . above the gateway; he was surrounded by himself."

On the ride to Saltsjobäden, Krogh makes a giant effort to smash through the wall of self that surrounds him and isolates him from his fellow man. Coming upon a railway bridge where work is going on in the headlight-illumined dark, Krogh has Anthony stop the car so that he may get out. As a very young man he had once worked on a bridge in Chicago. Why he had been happy then and why he had had friends, he could not now remember. "He could remember only these things: ice on the lake, a room in an apartment house with a hammock bed, the bridge on which he worked, and how one night when it snowed he had bought a hot dog at a street corner and ate it under an arch out of the wind's way." It was to recover what these things stand for that Krogh "stood awkwardly beside the car in his evening dress, his fur coat over his arm," pathetically eager to talk with the workmen, to enter their world again. But the workmen, laughing good-naturedly and talking gently, "allied together against the cold and dark, against death in the falling bolt, in faulty metal, in the frayed rope," take no notice of the unhappy tycoon.

This incident is an eye opener for Kate Farrant, who previously took Krogh at his own valuation. She thought of him as the future, as self-sufficient. But the sight of him now, standing forlorn on the tracks, silently begging the workmen to recognize that he was once one of them, convinces her that she was mistaken. She realizes for the first time that he is no different from Anthony and herself—insecure, isolated, and lonely. The only time Kate does not feel lonely in her isolation is when Anthony is about. "It was the nearest she could get to completeness, having him in the same room, arguing, bullying, retreating." For his sake she manages everything: she makes the ambitious ascent into Krogh's orbit, where she doubles as his right hand and his mistress—even though Anthony is the only man she could ever love. After Kate secures a position in Stockholm for Anthony as Krogh's bodyguard, she tells herself: "I never looked back. Plotted for this, planned for this, saved for this, that we should be together again." Her spirit rejoices: "It was the culmination of all her plans, to have him there, making himself at home beside her desk, a home from home."

Kate's frantic efforts to help Anthony are based on feelings bordering on incest. As children they had a strange telepathic communion: one knew what the other thought; experienced what the other felt. Once at boarding school when Anthony screamed uncontrollably after sustaining a cut below his eye, when a knife he was using to skin a rabbit slipped, Kate, fifty miles away, woke in the middle of the night, heard him, and knew he was in pain. "He was pain, because she had never felt pain except through him." But as a result of her role as Krogh's mistress, Kate gradually forfeits this telepathic contact and this unusual sensitivity to Anthony's pain. A sense of guilt, as well as this abnormal relationship, is behind her frenzied efforts to protect him from the world and from himself. This feeling of guilt can be traced back to another schoolboy escapade. When Anthony wrote to Kate that he was running away from school, she intercepted him in a barn, halfway between their schools, at two o'clock in the morning, and persuaded him to return. Regretting having sent him "back from the barn to conform, to pick up the conventions, the manners, of all the rest," she later tries to undo the damage by plying him with security, by attempting to "build up his London inside the glass walls of Krogh's."

Anthony Farrant is more loved than lover in this abnormal brother-sister relationship. There is nothing Kate would not do for him, but there are things he would not do for her. Anthony does not bitterly envy lovers their more nearly complete alliance, as she does. She is incapable of loving anyone else, but "his love was blurred, was dispersed, was thinned out like pastry over a large area. Love was not gratitude, love was not this dependence of the brain, this thought-reading, this inconvenience of shared pain, this was the unfortunate trick of being twins; love was fun, love was a good time, love was Annette, was Mabel." In Stockholm, love was Lucia Davidge, a British girl travelling with her parents. Loo's very limited experience in affairs of the heart, which she exaggerates to give her a worldly air, is plainly revealed by her naïveté and her innocence, unintentionally self-exposed.

Anthony conducts a love affair to the accompaniment of tall stories designed to inflate his ego and make people like him. He has an inordinate desire to have people think well of him because of a lack of self-confidence which he strives desperately to conceal. This is manifest in his initial meeting with Krogh. "Then at the sound of a key turning in the hall door he momentarily lost his confidence. This was the price he had paid for his freshness, his schoolboy air of knowing a thing or two; he lived in the moment and was never prepared for the sudden crisis, the stranger's face, the new job." People who make Anthony feel inferior, he never forgives; nor people, like Krogh, to whom he owes gratitude. Perhaps his ultimate decision to desert Kate and follow Loo back to England is dictated in part by the fact that he owes gratitude to his twin sister and has a feeling of inferiority toward her. Also Anthony decides to leave Kate for Loo, because, unlike Kate, she flatters his vanity and is never "daunted at the sight of him in his suspect smartness, his depraved innocence, hopelessly unprepared in his old school tie." The itch of the flesh thus wins out over "the common life, telepathy at daybreak, the scar below his eye."

Anthony's affair with Loo is only physical. It means nothing to him spiritually. During their assignation in Minty's flat, "his mind remained apart, working a trick, conscious of the house group over her head, the Madonna on the mantelpiece, peacocking himself when she cried, 'I don't want you to go. I don't want you to go.'" Anthony is immature, not by reason of physical innocence but by a kind of childish numbness. "He had a child's cunning in a world of cunning men." He fornicates to gain adult power— "one liked to make them helpless"—to lose the isolation and insecurity of arrested youth, and to flatter his insatiable vanity. "It was vanity only which he experienced in the final act, it had never been anything else but vanity." The sense of being lifted out of himself, the destruction of spiritual isolation, he never experiences in the final act. Since he is out of touch with humankind, his sexual pleasure is always tainted. "His passion wore itself out in his hands."

The sexual relationship between Loo and Anthony is typical of so many such relationships in Greene's books. The sexual act gratifies the female far more than the male. Anthony knew "there was no pleasure to match theirs, which was deep enough to make them surrender momentarily every mental conviction, so that Loo now used all the terms she scouted; she said, 'I love you'; she said, 'Darling'; she said, 'It was never so good.'" And so it is in all the early novels: Lucy derives greater pleasure than Andrews; Kay derives more satisfaction than any of her many consorts. Vanity interferes with Anthony's gratification, guilt with Conrad's, and puritanism with Andrews'. Certain heroines of Greene not only experience greater emotion and passion than do his heroes, but are also less burdened down with a sense of guilt. Their attitude toward sex is the attitude expressed by the ribald woman young Andersen meets on the train. She speaks of sex, much to Andersen's embarrassment, as though it is "something not to be blushed at or hidden, something cheerful, common, careless, come today and gone tomorrow."

All these widely different characters are related by a common factor: they are trapped into life situations that defeat them, situations they do not understand, generated by their own dark pasts. Krogh is a victim of deadening worldly acedia. Kate and Anthony are victims of thirty-odd years in common. Minty is no exception: he is victim of an everlasting schoolboy complex. "The school and he were joined by a painful reluctant coition, a passionless coition that leaves everything to regret, nothing to love, everything to hate, but cannot destroy the idea: we are one body." He is a disillusioned ex-Harrow student eking out a pitiable existence as a shabby newspaper reporter in Stockholm. His job is to boswell Krogh, chronicle his comings and goings; Krogh's every move is news. Minty lives alone in one dingy room on the top floor of a boarding house. A Harrow dormitory photograph hangs above his ascetic bed. Minty does not appear in the picture; when it was taken, he was ill. The house group, minus Minty, is thus a symbolical reminder of his absence from the rush and hurl of life. He misers prep-school mementos: the uneaten chocolate bar, preserved for years, given him by a schoolmate; "the Brownie snap of himself with a butterfly net taken by" a second; "a copy of *The Bushman's Vade-Mecum*" given him by a third. All these "he kept as carefully as he would have kept the relic of saints, the Saxon thigh bone, the holy bandied splinter itself."

After prep school Minty somehow loses the knack of making friends. Anthony is the only friend he has thereafter. In a rare moment of self-knowledge, Anthony understands what drew them together:

He saw himself and Minty clearly as one person: the exile from his country and his class, the tramp whose workhouses were Shanghai, Aden, Singapore, the refuse of a changing world. If Minty were to be envied at all, it was that he had chosen his dump and stayed there. They hadn't the resources to hold their place, but the world had so conditioned them that they hadn't the vigour to resist. They were not fresh enough, optimistic enough, to believe in peace, co-operation, the dignity of labour, or if they believed in them, they were not young enough to work for them. They were neither one thing nor the other; they were really only happy when they were together: in the clubs in foreign capitals, . . . at old boys' dinners, momentarily convinced by the wine they couldn't afford that they believed in something: in the old country, in the king, . . . in the comradeship of the trenches.

On the strength of this and similar passages, commentators, such as Kenneth Allott, Arthur Calder-Marshall, and Jacques Madaule,[15] like to point out the following likenesses between Minty and Anthony: their public school background, their disillusionment, their failures, their status as socially displaced persons, their secret loyalties to past traditions, their nostalgia for England, their sense of isolation, and immature outlook. All these are valid, of course, but there are important differ-

[15] Allott, *op. cit.*, p. 104; Arthur Calder-Marshall, "The Works of Graham Greene," *Horizon*, May 1940, p. 368; Jacques Madaule, *Graham Greene* (Paris, Editions du Temps Présent, 1949), p. 34.

ences too, and it is these that are never pointed out. Minty
stopped living after prep school; Anthony started living after
prep school. Minty cherishes mementos of school, because he
came closer to happiness there than anywhere else; Anthony
wears a fake Harrow necktie, because it gives him false confidence and enables him to use people and promote deals.
Minty is a sedentary introvert resigned to defeat; Anthony is
a nomadic extrovert often convinced that one day his luck will
turn. Minty is a misogynist, and the ladies shun him; Anthony
is a lady's man, and the ladies adore him. In a restaurant, Kate
observes that her brother is "the mark of every waitress in
the room."

Minty loathes the human body. "Yes, it was ugly, the
human figure. Man or woman, it made no difference to Minty.
The body's shape, the running nose, excrement, the stupid
postures of passion, these beat like a bird's heart in Minty's
brain," stirring his malice. Minty's own body is ugly—
"crooked and yellow and pigeon-chested"—and has given him
great pain—"his stomach would bear nothing hot." He finds
the human figure so disgusting that he almost vomits "to think
that God Himself had become man. Minty could not enter
a church without the thought . . . which was more to him
than the agony in the garden, the despair upon the cross. Pain
was an easy thing to bear beside the humiliation which rose
with one in the morning and lay down with one at night."
Distorted idealism is responsible for Minty's fanatical hatred
of the human body.[16] For normal sexual expression, which is
abhorrent to him, he substitutes sadistic behavior in an effort
to relieve his own misery. This is reflected in the torture he
inflicts on a crippled spider trapped under his tooth-glass. But
in bed, at night, the situation is reversed and Minty becomes

[16] Allott, *op. cit.*, p. 110.

the victim: "his body stretched doggo in the attitude of death, he lay there humbly tempting God to lift the glass."

The plot that involves the central figures in each of these early novels is fairly constant. *The Shipwrecked* presents it in archetype. Anthony is a blustering braggart who is unable to adjust at school or later on a job. He is worried by a vague sense of impending disaster which he foresees as a consequence of his feeling nowhere at home. But disaster actually comes in the person of Fred Hall, Krogh's henchman, who, alarmed lest Anthony betray Krogh, murders him. Kate is the one, all along, who tries to divert threats to her brother's well-being and shore up his existence. The inability to adapt is crucial. Andrews could not adapt at school nor on his father's ship. Conrad is as much a misfit as chief clerk as he had been in school. The sense of disaster is also crucial and the quarter from whence disaster comes equally misunderstood. Andrews sees Carlyon as his nemesis; his self-destruction is really wrought by shameful compromises detrimental to "the man within." Conrad believes he has to fear the Commissioner; actually he should fear his subconscious desire to punish himself for his adultery. The theme of the trapped man who turns to a sympathetic woman for help and intercession recurs, too. Andrews finds semi-salvation to the extent of his loyalty to Elizabeth; Conrad dooms himself because he betrays Milly. "This preoccupation with betrayal, whether of a man by himself or of one man by another, together with its opposite quality of loyalty, runs through Greene's earlier novels."[17]

The points of resemblance among the characters are even more pronounced than the similarities in plot. The trapped

---

[17] Walter Allen, "Graham Greene," *Writers of Today*, ed. D. Baker (London, Sidgwick, 1946), p. 22.

man's childhood relations with his family are always important to an understanding of his adult behavior. Andrews inherited his father's cowardice; Conrad detested the pretentious
name fastened on him by his parents; Anthony was caught up
in Kate's darkness. All three had sad childhoods. All three are
explained in terms of their unhappy schooldays. (Their common hatred of school echoes Greene's own hatred of school—
as developed at length in the first chapter.) School repressed
Andrews' romantic instincts; fellow schoolboys taunted Conrad for his brains; school taught Anthony only how to
prolong his adolescence. They were doomed from their
schooldays, betrayed by what they made of themselves. In
this unhappy state of mind, the communication of persons
with one another becomes a problem. They cannot give themselves where they most want to. Andrews cannot communi-
cate with Carlyon; Conrad and Anthony with anyone at all.
None of them feels as if he belongs anywhere. They are all
in exile: Andrews from his seafaring companions; Conrad from
his family and co-workers; Anthony from his social class.
They all have a nagging sense of inferiority. Andrews feels
inferior to Carlyon; Conrad to his brother; Anthony to Krogh.
They all come to a violent end: Andrews by his own hand;
Conrad under the wheels of an automobile; Anthony by
drowning. The plot and the characters are saved from repetition by the tempo of the story, the complex insight of the
author, and the fact that the trapped-man formula is varied
with each novel.

These characters have produced progeny aplenty in
Greene's later works. Carlyon, like the Hyde Park soapbox
orator, Smythe, in *The End of the Affair*, seeks a compensation for his disfigured face by dreaming dreams. Mrs. Butler,
the housekeeper in *The Man Within*, with her "flippant

streaks of yellow hair," her "ample breasts," and her wide experience of men, foreshadows Ida Arnold, the buxom blonde tart in *Brighton Rock*. The heroine of *The End of the Affair*, Sarah Miles, who undergoes a metamorphosis from slut to saint, is a composite of Lucy and Elizabeth, the bad and the good angel. Mrs. Coney, the wife of the slain policeman in *It's a Battlefield*, is the first of a recurrent type—the perennial victim who is forever taken advantage of because he never asserts himself. This type recurs in the person of Sarah Miles' husband, Henry, who is tolerant to a fault where his wife's lover is concerned. Jules Briton, the café waiter in *It's a Battlefield* and the first Catholic in the Greene canon, has multiple descendants in the Catholic novels. Minty, with his fear of women and the sex act, his arrested puberty, his bitter virginity, his sadism, his religious sense, is the first draft of Pinkie, the boy gangster in *Brighton Rock*. Minty's unhappy schooldays parallel the equally unhappy schooldays of Harris and Wilson in *The Heart of the Matter*. The English dentist Tench, in *The Power and the Glory*, is a miserable exile like Minty. The ruthless Fred Hall is the first of a series of diabolists and nihilists: Raven in *This Gun For Hire;* Willi Hilfe in *The Ministry of Fear;* Harry Lime in *The Third Man;* Pinkie in *Brighton Rock;* the Police Lieutenant in *The Power and the Glory;* and from *Twenty-One Stories,* Fred and Blacker.

3 The Entertainments

I

GRAHAM GREENE has been writing "entertainments" over a long period of time. *Orient Express*, his first "entertainment," appeared in 1932; *Our Man in Havana*, his most recent one, appeared in 1958. In between, he produced *This Gun For Hire* (1936), *The Confidential Agent* (1939), *The Ministry of Fear* (1943), *The Third Man* (1950), and *Loser Takes All* (1955). The fact that he has ceased to produce entertainments since 1958 does not diminish their importance in the corpus of his works.

Greene divides his fiction into novels, entertainments, short stories, and plays. Only the first two categories are likely to cause any confusion. His entertainments can be distinguished from his novels by a greater use of melodrama, by a comparative lack of development in the characters, and by a concession to the happy ending. In an essay praising Henry James, Greene draws a distinction between drama and melodrama which also illustrates the difference between Greene's novels and entertainments. "The novel by its nature is dramatic, but it need not be melodramatic, and James's problem was to admit violence without becoming violent. He mustn't let violence lend the tone (that is melodrama): violence must draw its tone from all the rest of life; it must be subdued, and it must not, above all, be sudden and inexplicable."[1] In general, violence, which is present in both the novel and the entertain-

[1] *The Lost Childhood*, p. 49.

ment—but to a far greater degree in the latter—lends tone to the entertainment, and if not always inexplicable in origin is always sudden in appearance. Treachery is the screw turned in both the novel and the entertainment, subject to this difference: in the former Greene sheds the more obvious melodramatic trappings of betrayal.

The exigencies of plot dictated by a heavy reliance on melodrama do not permit very much character development. Hence in the entertainment, Greene is forced to focus his attention on a few characters and allow the rest to stand as a backset for the melodrama he is staging. If some of the characters in an entertainment have to be archetypal and seen more in silhouette than in the round, there are nonetheless compensations. Whether it be a nightmarish catastrophe, a vertiginous chase, or hallucinatory coincidence, the machinery of Greene's suspense melodramas never creaks. These psychological thrillers—for that is what most of the entertainments really are—feature a subtlety of perception, an ingenuity of situation, an immediate and lasting sense of suspense, a swiftness of narrative pace, and a mastery of style that even his most competent detective-story rivals find hard to match. Where the entertainment has to defer to the novel, ultimately, is in the area where the reader is affected. None of the thrillers disturbs the reader's complacency nor drugs him with powerful, long-lasting after-effects, as the novels do. This is the price the thriller has to pay for subordinating the interrelations between character and circumstance to high-speed narrative tempo.

In a critical revaluation of *The Portrait of a Lady* and *The Wings of the Dove*, Greene suggests that James' "ruling passion, . . . the idea of treachery, the 'Judas complex,' "[2] made a happy ending impossible. "There is no way out of the

[2] *Ibid.*, p. 44.

inevitable betrayal except the way that Milly Theale . . . took involuntarily."[3] Since the innocent figure in Greene's books is likewise destined for betrayal and violent death, Greene's novels also have sad endings. But Greene indicates in the preface to *The Third Man* his preference in an entertainment for a happy ending. The happy ending in the entertainment—more apparent, to be sure, than real—deserves this designation only by comparison with the grimmer issue in the novel. For even when lovers are brought together in the final chapter—Anne Crowder and Jimmy Mather, Rose Cullen and D., Anna Hilfe and Arthur Rowe, Anna Schmidt and Rollo Martins—their happiness is shadowed, and they are not allowed to expect much from life. Still this represents a compromise with the conventional thriller, something Greene is less inclined to do in his novels.

Enumerating the chief differences between the novel and the entertainment only serves to raise a more fundamental question: why does Greene, unlike most other serious novelists, write entertainments at all? Is it because he must? At least he himself thinks so. "I couldn't help smiling to think of the many readers who have asked me me why I sometimes write thrillers, as though a writer chooses his subject instead of the subject choosing him. It sometimes seems as though our whole planet had swung into the fog belt of melodrama, but, perhaps, if one doesn't ask questions, one can escape the knowledge of the route we are on. . . ."[4] A generation ago, he observes in *The Ministry of Fear*, melodrama "about spies, and murders, and violence, and wild motorcar chases" seemed synthetic. Now these things, no longer devices of melodrama,

[3] *Ibid.*, p. 43.
[4] "Catholic Temper in Poland," *Atlantic Monthly*, March 1956, p. 39.

belong to the modern world of barbarism and terrorism, which Greene understands well:

Today our world seems peculiarly susceptible to brutality. There is a touch of nostalgia in the pleasure we take in gangster novels, in characters who have so agreeably simplified their emotions that they have begun living again at a level below the cerebral. We, like Wordsworth, are living after a war and a revolution, and these half-castes fighting with bombs between the cliffs of skyscrapers seem more likely than we to be aware of Proteus rising from the sea.[5]

Unlike Edgar Wallace's old-fashioned thrillers, Graham Greene's modern thrillers expose, in addition to a murderer, a profound problem. Like Chesterton, Greene uses the detective story to dramatize a moral problem of far-reaching significance. Greene's Ishmaelites are so alive to the immense combat of heaven and hell that they are doubly pursued. On the narrative level, Czinner, Raven, D., Rowe, and Harry Lime are marked and hunted by the police, the Fascists, the Nazis, or the Communists. On the psychological level, they are hounded and scarred by what Mary McCarthy calls "the Eumenides of conscience, by guilt, by the loss of God, the sense of moral implication in the crime that is the modern world."[6] By placing the moral problem at the core of the narrative, Greene modernizes the standard thriller. According to Morton Zabel, "Greene has brought about one of the most promising collaborations between realism and spirituality that have recently appeared in fiction, saving his work as much from the squashy hocus-pocus or mechanical contrivance of

[5] *Journey Without Maps*, p. 10.
[6] "Graham Greene and the Intelligentsia," *Partisan Review*, XI (Spring 1944), 229.

the common thriller as from the didactic sanctimony of conventional religiosity."[7]

In associating morality with the traditional detective story, Greene follows the example of Dostoyevsky in *Crime and Punishment*. Before the murder of the old pawnbroker, Raskolnikov considers himself emancipated from the moral law; after the murder, his tormented conscience forces him to acknowledge his dependence upon the law of God. The spiritually dislocated characters of Greene's entertainments are also driven, or at least tempted, to ally themselves with the law-abiding. The problem of identity confounds Raskolnikov, for he has two identities, one projected as Svidrigailov. His split personality debases him until Sonia shows him the way to attain a single, unified identity. Greene's heroines similarly serve as oases of love in the desert of abandonment for those of his heroes who have a dual personality. While Andrews is the most obvious example, none of Greene's heroes is entirely free from the torment of a disordered personality.

The greatest achievement in the twentieth-century English thriller is Joseph Conrad's *The Secret Agent* (1907). The matter of the novel, as F. R. Leavis points out, is that of standard melodrama— "terrorist conclaves, embassy machinations, bomb-outrage, detection, murder, suicide"—but "in treating such matters with all the refinements of his craft,"[8] Conrad makes *The Secret Agent* the classic of its genre. This masterpiece could easily have been at least a remote inspiration for *The Confidential Agent* (1936).[9] *The Secret Agent* is

[7] "Graham Greene," *Forms of Modern Fiction*, ed. William Van O'Connor (Minneapolis, Minnesota University Press, 1948), p. 293.

[8] *The Great Tradition* (New York, Doubleday, 1954), p. 254.

[9] Greene holds Conrad in high regard, but he does not specifically mention *The Secret Agent*.

based upon the fact that a Russian *agent provocateur* had attempted in 1894 to blow up the Greenwich Observatory as a means of arousing British indignation against the Nihilists. It tells of a secret agent in the employ of a foreign embassy in London and of his relations with his employers, with anarchists, with the police, and with his own family. *The Confidential Agent*, based upon the fact that during the Spanish civil war both sides tried to obtain from England an exclusive trade agreement to buy coal, tells of a confidential agent in the employ of the Communists in London and of his relations with a treacherous embassy, with fellow Communists, with rival agents, with Scotland Yard, and with the memories of his dead wife.

Conrad is now recognized as a pioneer in having put melodrama to serious use in the British novel. In *Under Western Eyes* (1911), for example, he uses melodrama to document Russian character and Russian history and to serve as an exemplum of his conviction that "the old despotism and the new Utopianism are complementary forms of moral anarchy."[10] Conrad's contemporary, Thomas Hardy, was also one of the first to couple a serious intention with melodrama. He employed melodrama, not for shock value nor for comic relief, but as a frame for his fatalistic philosophy and for the interweaving of environment and character. "The President of the Immortals" sports with Tess Durbeyfield amidst all kinds of melodramatic trappings. In using melodrama for a serious purpose, Greene follows both Conrad and Hardy. But he is more like Conrad than Hardy in treating melodramatic themes subtly, whereas Hardy overworked hackneyed plot-

[10] *Under Western Eyes* (New York, New Directions, 1951), p. xxvii.

devices—such as unexpected meetings, undivulged secrets, and undelivered messages.

Greene has an interest in Conrad's kind of human being. Conrad's interest was not in the typical person but in the exceptional one. Greene's imagination is also captured by moral heroism or moral degradation. *Orient Express*, for instance, contrasts the fundamental heroism of Coral Musker and Dr. Czinner with the essential degradation of Mabel Warren and Quin Savory. Cautious mediocrity, which annoyed Conrad, also provokes Greene's contempt. Although the best examples of this are to be found in the Catholic novels (the pious woman in *The Power and the Glory*) and plays (Aunt Helen in *The Living Room*), the hectic life that all Greene's heroes and heroines lead is an implicit repudiation of caution and mediocrity. Studies in hopeless degeneration intrigued Conrad. Cases of puzzling mental pathology, like that of Willi Hilfe in *The Ministry of Fear* and Harry Lime in *The Third Man*, fascinate Greene.

Raven, the harelipped killer, in *This Gun For Hire*; D., the scholar turned confidential agent, in *The Confidential Agent*; and Arthur Rowe, the pitying mercy killer, in *The Ministry of Fear* are the most carefully delineated heroes of Greene's entertainments. Their motivations and emotions deserve close scrutiny.

In the long view, Raven is the raw material from which Pinkie, the boy gangster in *Brighton Rock*, is fashioned. Both Raven and Pinkie have bitter childhood memories: memories of stomach-turning squalor, unrelieved misery, and inhuman cruelty. Pinkie's childhood recollections of brutality and violence—his enforced presence on Saturday nights at the love-making of his parents, and the shocking suicide of a fifteen-year-old girl neighbor, pregnant out-of-wedlock—are mild by comparison with Raven's—his father hanged; his mother a suicide. "Hell lay about them in their infancy."[11] Evil stalked the nursery, and they grew up with the stench of corruption in their nostrils. Embittered by the theft of happiness in the cradle and the too early death of innocence, they nurse a grudge against life and share a need of destruction which makes them fearless and reckless. Mistrusting women, they have contempt for them. They are puritanical about sex and cynical about maternal love. Their obsessive preoccupation with betrayal makes them shrink from human contact, prone to believe that deception is the natural consequence of trust.

Raven has been shaped by hatred. "He had never felt the least tenderness for anyone; he was made in this image, and he had his own odd pride in the result; he didn't want to be unmade." Experience has made it impossible for him to love. Every attempt at love has ended in betrayal. Whenever he gives himself he is double-crossed: by his father, his mother, even by his own kind—the lawless. So he gradually associates loving, even communicating with others, with going soft, with exposing himself to jail or to a razor in the guts. He is constantly on the defensive against people who draw back in horror from his harelip. His deformity sours him until he hates the whole world, because the world cannot see beyond a man's face.

The greatest temptation Raven feels he has to resist is the impulse to trust another human being. Every time he trusts he suffers the pain of another betrayal. That is his tragedy. Yet dimly he realizes that the need to have faith in someone else is

[11] *Another Mexico*, p. 5.

basic, and so reluctantly he yields to the impulse to trust Anne Crowder, who ironically is the girl of the detective in pursuit of Raven. Only then does Raven lower the tremendous barrier of self-defense he has raised against his ugliness. With Anne in the railway shed he is, for the first time in his life, friendly, happy, hopeful, and self-confident—despite the presence of the police outside in the dark, foggy railroad yard. When his impulse to trust Anne is repaid, like every other act of faith he has ever made, by betrayal, it seals irrevocably his belief that "there was no one outside your own brain whom you could trust—not a doctor, not a priest, not a woman." Only for the briefest moment, just before he dies, is he even tempted to trust again. " 'Ah, Christ, that it were possible,' but he had been marked from his birth for this end, to be betrayed in turn by everyone until every avenue into life was safely closed: by his mother bleeding in the basement, by the chaplain at the home, . . . by the shady doctor off Charlotte Street. How could he have expected to escape the commonest betrayal of all, to go soft on a skirt?"

This Gun for Hire, reflecting the twentieth century's interest in political assassinations with international repercussions, was foreshadowed, as we have seen, by Conrad's *Under Western Eyes*. A parent classic in this genre, *Under Western Eyes* gave birth to the type of fiction that Greene carries to such extravagant lengths. Political assassination is a minor theme and the political assassin is a minor character in *Under Western Eyes*. Haldin, the student revolutionist who kills a Czarist official, and Raven are terrorists. The major similarity between the two works is that the assassination is modelled upon an actual sensational event. Conrad took the assassination of V. K. Plehve, Russian minister of the interior, in 1904, as his model. Greene used Zaharoff and the alliance between arma-

ments-manufacturing and *Machtpolitik* for a point of depart-
ture.

D., the hero of *The Confidential Agent*, is more intelligent,
more intellectual, and better educated than Raven, but he too
is afflicted with mistrust and hatred. D's hatred differs from
Raven's in that D.'s is largely confined to self-hatred.

In many respects, D. is the forerunner of Major Scobie, the
sensitive police officer in *The Heart of the Matter*. Like him,
D. is "haunted . . . by the vision of an endless distrust." Trust-
ing nobody but themselves, they sometimes are uncertain
whether they can even trust themselves. Their lack of self-
confidence is contagious, for no one else has confidence in
them. D.'s party continually keeps a check on him for fear
he should defect to the other side, and Scobie's superiors by-
pass him when a promotion is due. This lack of confidence is
ironical, since loyalty is natural to them. They are both frustrated by memories of the dead. Having "a dead wife on the
tongue," D. is unable to talk of love to any other woman.
Feeling guilty about ever loving again, he pities Rose Cullen.
Scobie's pity for his wife stems from his guilt at not having
been present when their only child died. This crippling sense
of responsibility to the country of the dead extends across the
frontier as well. D., unlike Scobie, does not carry responsibility
to the point where he is prepared to risk damnation for others,
but he is prepared to give his life. D., like Scobie, expresses a
death-wish: he longs to belong to history, with "all the struggle and violence over, wars decided one way or another, out
of pain."

D.'s near self-hatred is rooted in the delusion that he was
somehow responsible for his wife's death, even though he was
in a military prison at the time she was taken hostage and
executed. D. feels that he brings bad luck to others. He even

feels responsible for "breaking up God knows what lives" and "for the deaths of strangers." It grieves him to think that danger and disaster go with him everywhere. When Else, a fourteen-year-old hotel chambermaid, loses her job on account of him, he is shocked. "It was as if he had been given a glimpse of the guilt which clings to all of us without our knowing it. None of us knows how much innocence we have betrayed." D.'s sense of guilt and his compulsive preoccupation with shattered innocence and betrayal are signs of "some terrible aboriginal calamity."[12]

D.'s obsession with war ("Bombing planes took flight from between his eyes, and in his brain the mountains shook with shell-bursts"); his suspicious nature ("People were united only by their vices; there was honour among adulterers and thieves"); his pessimism ("It was as if the whole world lay in the shadow of abandonment"); his fixation on pain and violence ("He felt homesick for the dust after the explosion, the noise of engines in the sky"); his fixation on death ("His territory was death; he could love the dead and the dying better than the living"); his passion for revenge ("Unless people received their deserts, the world to him was chaos"); and his sexual short-circuit ("The act of desire remained an act of faith, and he had lost his faith") are further by-products of original sin.

In tracing D.'s literary lineage we are apt to think immediately of Verloc, the police spy, in *The Secret Agent*. But the connection is a poor one; their characters are different. D. is high-minded, humble, and magnanimous towards the innocent and the helpless. Squalid and egotistical, Verloc exploits the innocent and the helpless. Axel Heyst (*Victory*, 1915),

---

[12] Greene took for his motto of *Another Mexico* a passage from Cardinal Newman. This quotation is from that passage.

another Conradian character, is actually the true progenitor of D. Their characters are similar. Sharing a profound mistrust of life, they deliberately choose to escape it—Heyst by drifting through the world as an onlooker; D. by withholding love. But they are both betrayed into action by casual acts of kindness, and more action is always the consequence of their action. Until the end, D. cannot believe in his happiness with Rose Cullen, any more than Heyst can believe in his happiness with Lena. Greene's admiration of *Victory*—one "of the great English novels of the last fifty years"[13]—may well explain the resemblance.

Lack of love and lack of trust are not entirely absent in Arthur Rowe, the hero of *The Ministry of Fear*, but they are subordinate to pity and sensitivity to pain. W. H. Auden calls attention to the fact that in the person of Arthur Rowe, "Graham Greene analyzes the vice of pity, that corrupt parody of love and compassion which is so insidious and deadly for sensitive natures." At bottom, pity is egotistical, for "behind pity for another lies self-pity, and behind self-pity lies cruelty." Auden thus briefly defines Rowe's ethic of pity.[14]

Greene does indeed expose pity as counterfeit charity. Even the counterfeiters, in lucid moments, know its true identity, as when Rowe admits that "pity is cruel. Pity destroys. Love isn't safe when pity's prowling around." When Rowe was driven by pity to destroy his wife, the newspapers called it a mercy killing, but they never said mercy to whom. "The law had taken a merciful view; himself he took the merciless one." He is shocked, when he finally stops rationalizing, to discover "that it was he who had not been able to bear his wife's pain—

[13] *The Lost Childhood*, p. 99.
[14] "The Heresy of Our Time," *Renascence*, I (Spring 1949), 24.

and not she. . . . It was her endurance and her patience which he had found most unbearable. He was trying to escape his own pain, not hers. . . . He could never tell whether she might not have preferred any sort of life to death." But then, as a Shavian character observes, "pity is the scavenger of misery."[15]

Rowe is very sensitive to pain. "It broke his precarious calm to feel that people suffered. Then he would do anything for them. Anything." He would even direct his sense of pity, that horrible and horrifying emotion, towards them, letting it roam around until it grew "to the monstrous proportions necessary to action." He does not willingly allow anything, however repulsive, to suffer. Once as a boy he beat a wounded rat to death because he could not endure its writhings. He is obsessed with the fear of another creature's pain, and he experiences a compulsion to remedy it at all costs. The death of his wife, the death of a rodent, the death of a bird—they are all one to Rowe. He kills more out of self-pity than pity: to save himself the agony of watching. "He was aware of something unhappy, something imprisoned at the bottom of the brain trying to climb out. It frightened him in the same way as birds frightened him when they beat up and down in closed rooms. There was only one way to escape that fear. . . . That was to lash out until the bird was stunned and quiet or dead."

Rowe's pity is spent only on the unhappy or the unsuccessful. When, on one occasion, Anna Hilfe's "face looked ugly in the attempt to avoid tears; it was an ugliness which bound him [Rowe] to her more than any beauty could have done. It isn't being happy together, he thought . . . , that makes one love—it's being unhappy together." And prior to this, when he was struggling to regain his memory, "it wasn't failure he

[15] *Major Barbara.*

feared nearly so much as the enormous tasks that success might confront him with." In this respect, Rowe is the precursor of Major Scobie, who thinks lovingly that even God is a failure. Pity, aroused by a hypersensitivity to the suffering of the weak, the victimized, the seedy, wrecks both their lives: it prompts Rowe to euthanasia and Scobie to adultery and suicide. Rowe and Scobie are betrayed and trapped by their excessive sympathy for the suffering of others, by their fixed response to the siren call of pain.

Where responsibility is concerned, Rowe is most like Scobie. Neither of them discharges his obligations lightly. This agonizing sense of responsibility also stems from their pity. One of the forms which Rowe's pity takes is the comforting lie, which conveniently pretends to ignore painful truths in order to postpone unhappiness. In the end when his recovery from amnesia is complete, when he discovers the whole sordid truth about his mercy killing, he deliberately withholds the information from Anna—who, ironically, has been perpetually on guard to shield him from it—to avoid causing her any further suffering. "He felt an enormous love for her, enormous tenderness, the need to protect her at any cost. She had wanted him innocent and happy. . . . He had got to give her what she wanted. Life had no other task for him." Scobie too assumes undue responsibility for the happiness of others. He lies to himself, to his wife, to his mistress.

Where consciousness of the link between pity and childhood is concerned, Rowe is least like Scobie. He is conscious of the process that bent the twig, whereas Scobie is totally ignorant of the origin of his pity. For this Greene must accept the responsibility: he chose to realize Rowe in the past as well as in the immediate present. Scobie is realized almost exclusively in the present. As an innocent child, Rowe has great expectations.

"In childhood we live under the brightness of immortality—heaven is as near and actual as the seaside. Behind the complicated details of the world stand the simplicities: God is good, the grown-up man or woman knows the answer to every question, there is such a thing as truth, and justice is as measured and faultless as a clock." This childish expectation is too soon tarnished by time and experience. "He learned before he was seven what pain was like. . . . He was often ill, his teeth were bad and he suffered agonies from an inefficient dentist he knew as Mr. Griggs." Grounded in the disillusionment of infantile hope, Rowe's adolescent pity has failed to mature into adult love.

Razumov, in *Under Western Eyes,* suffers from self-pity. He confesses to Natalia: "I've never known any kind of love." But it is not for this reason alone that Rowe deserves to be likened to him. There are many other resemblances. Neither of them has any relatives or friends; neither has the moral courage to resist a temptation to treachery (Razumov betrays a young revolutionary); and neither is able to justify his treachery to himself, despite repeated attempts to do so. Both are trapped by guilt; both give their lives over to redeeming their acts of cowardice (like Lord Jim); both work out their destiny through love extended to them by the sisters of the very men they defeat. The area of conflict is where they differ, however. While Razumov is largely in conflict with himself, Rowe adds conflict with the Ministry of Fear to self-conflict.

The most important way in which Rowe resembles Razumov is the way in which nearly all of Greene's heroes resemble Conrad's. Razumov is almost perpetually in a state of social and moral quarantine. "He was as lonely in the world as a man swimming in the deep sea. The word Razumov was the mere label of a solitary individuality." Rowe is doomed to endure a tormented conscience in utter loneliness. "It wasn't only that he had no money: he had no longer what he called a home—somewhere to shelter from people who might know him." Razumov is what the Conradian hero invariably is: an "outsider" with a sense of being in exile. Also called Kurtz, Jim, and Heyst, he catches the conscience of modern man in search of affirmation. Rowe is what Greene's hero invariably is: a solitary with a sense of never belonging. Also called Czinner, Raven, and D., he holds the mirror up to modern man in search of belief.

There is greater uniformity among Greene's heroines than among his heroes. Coral Musker, the chorus girl, in *Orient Express;* Anne Crowder, the chorus girl, in *This Gun for Hire;* Rose Cullen and Else, the rich girl and poor girl respectively, in *The Confidential Agent;* Anna Hilfe, the Austrian refugee, in *The Ministry of Fear;* and Anna Schmidt, the Hungarian refugee, in *The Third Man* are much alike with respect to appearance, character traits, and mission in life.

Anne Crowder recalls Coral Musker in appearance, occupation, and temperament. Coral and Anne are thin chorus girls with small features and pretty figures. They are afraid of one thing only: the insecurity of show-girl life. "The agents, the long stairs, the landladies" frighten Coral. Anne is "scared of the new faces and the new job, the harsh provincial jokes, the fellows who were fresh." They are unusually courageous, cheerful, ingenious, surprisingly innocent, and willing to make the best of things. Because of their generosity, their impulsiveness, they are often mistakenly regarded by men as pushovers. But their true relationship with men is basically a spiritual one. Their mission is to swerve the outcast from bitter solitude, to comfort the seedy. Coral's devotion to Dr. Czinner brings the dying political leader self-knowledge and a sense of peace. Anne's devotion to Raven brings the rejected boy sympathy, a respite from his long loneliness, and, temporarily at least, an end to the search for lost innocence.

Rose Cullen's childhood was set against a background of homelessness, her father's unscrupulous business associates, his mistresses, private detectives, and mistrust. Else's childhood is spent in a one-night cheap hotel. Despite their youth and their knowledge of human turpitude, they manage to retain their innocence and their faculty of belief. Staking all on love, Rose risks everything for D. So does Else, who "had all the innocence of a life passed since birth with the guilty." D. is profoundly shocked by knowledge of the corruption that Rose and Else have acquired so prematurely. "You learned too much in these days before you came of age. His own people knew death before they could walk; they got used to desire early—but this savage knowledge that ought to come slowly, the gradual fruit of experience. . . . In a happy life the final disillusionment with human nature coincided with death. Nowadays they seemed to have a whole lifetime to get through somehow after it."

Coral and Anne, who also combine innocence and experience, bear a resemblance to Rose and Else, although they have no counterpart of D. to be haunted by their spoilt youth and their precocious awareness of evil. All four are small, bony, and worried, wearing fidelity like a mask and capable of loyalty to anyone with whom they find something in common. They are all caught up in other people's violence, invariably pitying and pitied by the men whose violence they share. Most of the time their reward for unselfishness and decency is shabby treatment. Despite this, never faltering, they continue to cherish notions about the basic goodness of mankind and to harbor secret dreams of love and security. As Allott observes, "Greene always romanticizes these girls, stressing their pathos and courage, the special appeal to him of their thinness and cheerfulness."[16]

What happiness there is in Greene's entertainments is usually jeopardized by the misgivings of his heroines. Anna Hilfe is uncertain that she has been able to arrest Rowe's recovery from amnesia short of the point where his complete memory returns and the culpability for euthanasia dawns on him. Rose Cullen is not at all sure that she can beget a new innocence in D. The spectre of Raven in the mind of Anne Crowder is doomed to cloud a little the happiness of Anne and Mather. Long on self-knowledge, these young women do not practice self-deception. They know they can interrupt isolation in the men they love, but they are disquieted by doubts about the permanence of the salvation they bring, the cure they produce, the therapy they administer, the balm they bestow. Greene's exalted heroines combine the offices of priest, doctor, psychiatrist, and medicine man.

Anna Schmidt, Harry Lime's girl, is an actress, small in stature like Coral Musker and Anne Crowder but, unlike them, stocky. Her face is not beautiful, any more than their faces are, but, like theirs, "it was a face to live with, day in, day out. A face for wear." In other ways, she also resembles them: where fellow human beings are concerned, she stands for tolerance and leaves a wide margin for belief. She advises Martins, "We've got to remember him [Lime] as he was to us. There are always so many things one doesn't know about a person, even a person one loves—good things, bad things. We have to leave plenty of room for them." Anna accepts people as they are. Angrily she tells Martins, "For God's sake stop

16 *The Art of Graham Greene*, p. 81.

making people in *your* image. Harry was real. He wasn't just your hero and my lover. He was Harry. He was in a racket. He did bad things. What about it? He was the man we knew."

In Greene's work, the idealized heroine plays the role of a mysterious and slightly blind instrument of Providence. Setting an example for the hero to follow, she teaches him to live courageously. Whenever the hero heeds the heroine, he is the better for it. This kind of heroine is a point of contact between Greene and a host of other novelists—notably Dostoyevsky and Conrad.

Sonia, the heroine of *Crime and Punishment*, is driven to a life of prostitution that she may save her family from starvation. But the murderer Raskolnikov, who has a holy esteem for righteous suffering, thinks she may be intrinsically pure enough to serve as the instrument of his atonement. He tests her by forcing her to read aloud to him the story of the raising of Lazarus. She does this so movingly that his belief in her is confirmed; he confesses the murder, and his atonement starts. This incident invites comparison with a similar incident involving Rose Cullen and D. At first he doubts that she means to help him. But as he gradually learns from her how to be faithful to the living without, at the same time, breaking any essential trust with the dead, he changes. "He . . . felt a tremendous gratitude that there was somebody in the warring crooked uncertain world he could trust besides himself. It was like finding in the awful solitude of a desert a companion." In works of this kind, the hero is often so dazed, so numb, that it takes the heroine a little time to get through to him.

Conrad's heroines often have to justify life to his heroes. Natalia of *Under Western Eyes* and Lena of *Victory* give transfusions of moral courage to Razumov and Heyst respectively. But the price is costly. Razumov pays with his hearing

—his eardrums deliberately burst by an anthropoid terrorist —when, out of love for Natalia, he confesses his treachery to her and to the revolutionists. Heyst pays with his life—he fires his bungalow and perishes in the flames—when, out of love for Lena, he pronounces his trust in life. These victories for life are thus as ironical as they are unequivocal. Razumov exchanges one kind of isolation for another: he exchanges moral isolation for the less intolerable isolation of stone-deafness; Heyst exchanges life for death at the moment of his greatest confidence in life. Although Greene's heroes sometimes die shortly after his heroines justify life to them—as in the cases of Dr. Czinner and Raven—Greene does not imply, as Conrad does in *Lord Jim* as well as in *Victory*, that a spiritual victory is necessarily a swift prelude to death.

In an essay on James, an essay on Dickens, and an essay on Fielding, in *The Lost Childhood*, Greene indicates his attitude towards villains. He approves of James' villains—"Mme Merle, Gilbert Osmond, Kate Croy, Merton Densher, Charlotte Stant"—and Dickens' villains—"Fagin, Monks and Sykes"— because they possess the sense of supernatural evil. He disapproves of Fielding's villains because "they completely lack the sense of supernatural evil. . . . Evil is always a purely sexual matter: the struggle seems invariably to take the form of whether or not the 'noble lord' or Colonel James will succeed in raping or seducing Amelia." Greene regards intense moral struggle as a *sine qua non* for supernatural evil, "and it is the intensity of the struggle which is lacking in Fielding." But Greene's entertainments do present an intense moral struggle, and the evil that enmeshes his villains is never a purely sexual matter. Willi Hilfe in *The Ministry of Fear* and Harry Lime in *The Third Man*, Greene's two outstanding villains, illustrate this perfectly. Greene's practice in this matter conforms to his theory.

Willi Hilfe and Harry Lime are the kind of villain Greene specializes in, utterly selfish amoralists who have lost the sense of the worth of human life. Lime organizes a vicious black market operation that culminates in mass murder in post-war Vienna during the occupation; Hilfe organizes espionage, terrorism, and murder in wartime London. Lime steals penicillin from military hospitals, dilutes it, and sells it for a very high sum to the children's hospital, for use against meningitis. Apprised that many children have been killed by his fake drugs, he merely shrugs the information off and boasts how he clears thirty thousand pounds a year, tax free.

Harry Lime and Willi Hilfe have about them the same diabolical quality as Mrs. Baines in "The Basement Room,"[17] Greene's most memorable short story. Mrs. Baines "was darkness when the night light went out in a draught; she was the frozen blocks of earth he had seen one winter in a graveyard when someone said, 'They need an electric drill'; she was the flowers gone bad and smelling in the little closet room at Penstanley. There was nothing to laugh about." Nor do Lime and Hilfe afford anyone anything to laugh about. Not ordinary criminals, they are ambitious, clever, educated, warped, and completely unscrupulous. They never think in terms of human beings; they can endure pain—other people's pain—endlessly, and they treat murder as a joke. Not old-fashioned murderers, killing from fear, from hate—least of all from love—they murder for position, for substantial profit—even to become respectable. They meet appropriately violent deaths: Hilfe in a public lavatory; Lime in a public sewer.

The Ministry of Fear, as organized by Willi Hilfe, is com-

[17] The English title is "The Fallen Idol."

posed of British sympathizers and supporters of the Nazis, engaged in espionage and sabotage in and around London during World War II. Willi solicits vulnerable people, people who have something to hide, people who have done something shabby in the past. He recruits all kinds—a psychoanalyst, a socialite, a tailor, a poet, a critic, a painter, a clergyman—by blackmail and coerces them into the service of Germany. Not only does Willi's Ministry of Fear get a hold on certain people, but it so contaminates public trust that mistrust infects everyone except "saints—or outcasts with nothing to lose." But there is another and more permanent Ministry of Fear whose aims are not limited to "winning a war or changing a constitution. It was a ministry as large as life to which all who loved belonged. If one loved one feared." Arthur Rowe is a charter member of the larger bureau.

The two Ministries of Fear wage war. The war, a secret undercover struggle, is between those who pity, those who cannot bear other people's pain, and the pitiless, those who care nothing for the pain of others. In the person of Willi Hilfe, Greene probes into the corners of pitilessness. Pity is ostensibly pitted against pain, Arthur Rowe against Willi Hilfe. But since they have murder in common, Rowe's pity is paradoxically no better than Willi's pain. Actually overdeveloped pity is matched against underdeveloped pity.

Willi is a nihilist: "not caring for anything, having no rules and feeling no love." He is like Nikita, the monstrous villain of *Under Western Eyes,* another "perfect flower of the terroristic wilderness." Economical, Willi believes in "the maximum of terror for the minimum time directed against the fewest objects"; Nikita too practices economy in the way he renders his victims harmless. With just two swings of his enormous arms he purposely bursts the drums of Razumov's ears. Nikita even looks the part of a villain—he is so grotesque as to set dogs barking at the mere sight of him—and in this respect he belongs to an old-fashioned literary tradition. Willi is more up-to-date. His appearance is disarming. With his pale blue eyes, his pale gold hair, his handsome face, and his charming manner, he appears to be an innocent youth.

Willi represents violence. "Wherever men killed, his spirit moved in obscure companionship." His last thoughts, before he dies, coincide with a London air raid. Envying the fun the German pilots are having up there, "He was like a mortally sick man saying farewell to the sports of his contemporaries: no fear, only regret. He had failed to bring off the record himself in destruction. Five people only were dead: it hadn't been much of an inning compared with what they were having up there."

In the 1930's, when Greene was writing his early entertainments, the violence that always accompanies radical social and political change was even greater than usual. His thrillers were barometers well suited to register the foulest weather of that stormy decade. They remind us of the moral and physical effects of violence in the modern world. As he himself has written, "Life is violent and art has to reflect that violence."[18] All Greene's characters expect violence; they cannot evade it. D. is typical in this respect. "This was the atmosphere in which he had lived for two years; if he had found himself on a desert island, he would have expected to infect even the loneliness somehow with violence." When Greene, writing in October 1940, also makes a moving confession of intimacy with violence, we realize that D., on this point at least, reflects his creator's mental processes:

[18] *The Lost Childhood*, p. 49.

Violence comes to us more easily because it was so long expected
—not only by the political sense but by the moral sense. The world
we lived in could not have ended any other way. The curious
waste lands one sometimes saw from trains—the cratered ground
round Wolverhampton under a cindery sky with a few cottages
grouped like stones among the rubbish: those acres of abandoned
cars round Slough; the dingy fortune-teller's on the first-floor
above the cheap permanent waves in a Brighton back street: they
all demanded violence, like the rooms in a dream where one knows
that something will presently happen—a door fly open or a
window-catch give and let the end in.[19]

Greene is well aware of the twentieth century's climate of
violence. Violence became a way of life for him and his fellow
Londoners during Armageddon, Part Two. "The nightly rou-
tine of sirens, barrage, the probing raider, the unmistakable
engine ('Where are you? Where are you? Where are you?'),
the bomb-bursts moving nearer and then moving away, hold
one like a love-charm."[20] And in his thrillers violence is presented as part of the human condition, that part from which
most of his heroes absent themselves once during the course of
the book so that they may undergo a change in character and
grow.

Greene often shows the development of character in a shed
of some kind. In the Subotica station shed, Dr. Czinner discovers that loyalty to an ideal, even at the expense of his life,
is preferable to craven expediency. In all his lonely life, the
only time Raven can really be what he longs to be as a man is
those moments spent with Anne in the Nottwich railway shed.
Crouched in a little wooden coal shed, in a tiny back garden
in a small mining town, D. thinks of his deceased wife, and
for the first time he feels "the tie weakening between him and

[19] *Ibid.*, p. 189.
[20] *Ibid.*, p. 190.

the grave." It is a moment of revelation not unlike the epiphanies to the dying Dr. Czinner in the Subotica station shed and the trapped Raven in the Nottwich railway shed. These characters take spiritual inventory in sheds, because these structures seem to be the only place where Czinner, Raven, and D. can pause from pursuit and obtain a cease-fire from violence.

This preoccupation with sheds as a haven from pursuit and as a place where the protagonist can review his past is not confined to the entertainments. For, at the beginning of his flight, Andrews, in *The Man Within*, waking up in a strange potting shed remembers with gratitude something from his childhood: the potting shed of his home where an old gardener extended to him the affection denied the boy by his unloving father. Again, a potting shed, in the play of the same name, assumes crucial significance in the childhood of the leading character. For thirty years, a neurotic fear of a potting shed on his father's estate has blighted James Callifer's life. He knows only that something strange beyond ordinary belief happened there when he was fourteen. When he finally finds out what it was —that he hanged himself and was saved by a miracle—he frees himself from his terror of the past.

Put Greene's characters in a shed and they suddenly become ten foot tall. There they realize their potentialities for growth as they are unable to anywhere else. They learn something about themselves that invariably adds to their stature. In sheds of one kind or another, minor miracles soften hardened individuals: Czinner finds the courage to be himself; Raven fulfills his need to confess to a sympathetic human being; D. rediscovers the ability to love; Andrews recalls in the midst of pain a happier time; and James Callifer solves the mystery of his attempted suicide. In short, Greene employs the shed as a device which permits his protagonists to shed their burdens, to emancipate themselves from whatever fetters them, at least temporarily. Perhaps the shed is the primitive equivalent of —even the novelist's intuitive shorthand for—the confessional and the psychoanalytic couch.

The central characters in Greene's entertainments always fall into one of two categories. The hero and the heroine are invariably loyal and unselfish. Those characters who oppose the hero and the heroine are invariably opportunistic and selfish. The antithesis is saved from mere mechanism by Greene's ingenuity and insight. The antithesis recurs in entertainment after entertainment: Raven and Anne against Sir Marcus, the conscienceless millionaire munitions-maker, and his equally unprincipled associate, Davis, in *This Gun for Hire;* D., Rose, and Else against L., K., and the hotel manageress in *The Confidential Agent;* Rowe and Anna against Willi Hilfe and his English dupe, Dr. Forester, in *The Ministry of Fear;* hero-worshipping Rollo Martins against his onetime idol, Harry Lime, in *The Third Man. Orient Express* (1932), Greene's earliest entertainment, presents this basic dualism most pointedly.

For the dying revolutionist Dr. Richard Czinner, passage on the Orient Express symbolizes a man's journey through life. In his last fever-ridden hours, "he saw the express in which they had travelled breaking the dark sky like a rocket. They clung to it with every stratagem in their power, leaning this way and leaning that, altering the balance now in this direction, now in that. One had to be very alive, very flexible, very opportunist." His mind clouds over, "and soon he was falling through endless space, breathless, with a windy vacancy in head and chest, because he had been unable to retain his foothold on what was sometimes a ship and at other times a comet,

the world itself, or only a fast train from Ostend to Istanbul."
By his loyalty to an ideal, by his failure to lean this way and
that, he feels he has lost his foothold on life. Chorus girl Coral
Musker, a fellow passenger on the Orient Express, is also betrayed by her faithfulness, by her disinclination to be more
opportunistic.

Orient Express presents a group of ill-assorted people inter-
acting on one another in a closed setting. Besides Dr. Czinner
and Coral, who is going to Constantinople to join a dancing
troupe, the passengers include shrewd Carleton Myatt, a
wealthy young Jewish merchant; lesbian Mabel Warren, a
foreign correspondent for a London newspaper; her erstwhile
companion Janet Pardoe; and Cockney novelist Q. C. Savory.
These others stand apart from Coral and Dr. Czinner: they
seize opportunities and exploit situations, whereas Coral and
Dr. Czinner are loyal to people who would be better served
by cunning. Orient Express is the world in microcosm. Coral
and Dr. Czinner represent the selfless minority who extend
fidelity and gratitude to those who deserve neither. Myatt,
Mabel, Janet, and Savory represent the selfish majority who
lack the qualities to justify the faithfulness and the reliability
of the former.

Coral, who has "schooled herself to accept responsibility,"
becomes successively the mistress of Myatt, the nurse of Dr.
Czinner, and the companion of Mabel Warren. The first night
out of Ostend, Myatt, strolling by the non-sleeping com-
partments in the second class, encounters Coral in the corridor.
He offers to light her cigarette and they start to converse.
When Coral, who has been fighting a fever, faints, Myatt in-
duces her to accept his first-class sleeper and spends the night
in the corridor. But the next night they share his sleeping
compartment. She yields her virginity to him out of gratitude,

not passion. "The mere thought of performing that strange act when she was not drunk as she supposed some women were, or passionate, but only grateful, chilled her more than the falling snow. She was not even certain how one went about it, whether it would be necessary to spend a whole night with him, to undress completely in the cold carriage."

When Coral cries out with pain and Myatt discovers that he is her first lover, he is so startled and so touched that "he would have left her if she had not held him to her with her hands, while she said in a voice of which snatches only escaped the sound of the engine: 'Don't go. I'm sorry. I didn't mean. . . .' " Myatt's elation at having been Coral's first lover quickly subsides after she is forcibly taken from the train at Subotica the next morning. True, he does make a futile effort to rescue her, but he is soon faithless. For a scant two days after he loses her, Myatt can boast that Coral cost him ten pounds, the price of a sleeping compartment, and can propose marriage to Janet. Contrast this with Coral's obstinate fidelity as she clings forever "to her last sight of him in the restaurant-car with his fingers caressing his gold cigarette case."

Dr. Czinner is as self-sacrificing as Coral. They put duty to others above duty to themselves. Coral and Dr. Czinner are the only two passengers on the Orient Express who are described as wearing mackintoshes. The wearing of a mackintosh is an outer sign of their inner resemblance and, at the same time, is also an outer sign of their spiritual distance from the other passengers. In two later entertainments, mackintoshes are worn by a small band of stammerers gathered together for public therapy, waiting for a miracle (*This Gun for Hire*); and by a whole host of hopefuls: soapbox orators in Hyde Park, unemployed coal miners, the guilt-stricken hero D., and two frightened men instrumental in D.'s safe return home (*The Confidential Agent*). In a still later entertainment, *The Ministry of Fear*, Arthur Rowe's isolation and loneliness are underlined by his pathetic habit of attending "cinemas at ten in the morning with other men in mackintoshes who had somehow to pass the time away." Mackintoshes are the un-official uniform of decent but essentially seedy people: people who are unsuccessful and unassured, who think depressing and inhibiting thoughts.[21]

Dr. Czinner is travelling to Belgrade to foment a revolution. Five years earlier, as head of the Social Democrats, he fled from Yugoslavia when the government tried to arrest him on trumped-up charges. He took political refuge in England, under an alias, working as a schoolteacher and awaiting a pro-pitious time to return. His arrival in Belgrade is designed to coincide with a Communist outbreak, but the actual outbreak, which takes place while he is en route and anticipates his appearance on the scene by a mere three days, is quickly suppressed. At first his hopes are dashed, and he falters on his proposed destination, but later he resolves to return home any-way, give himself up, and stand trial with the imprisoned agitators. The world, he trusts, will then listen to his defense as it would never listen to him safe in England. But he never gets to Belgrade: he is taken from the train at Subotica, court-martialed in a matter of a few hours, and sentenced to death. Coral is detained at the same time, charged falsely with being Dr. Czinner's accomplice. When Dr. Czinner is wounded in an attempt at escape, Coral stops to assist him, deliberately forfeiting her own excellent chance to get away. She drags

[21] A mackintosh is a common symbolic device. When worn by a character of Joyce's or Woolf's, for example, a mackintosh is meant to insulate the wearer against reality, to keep life out. Greene's use of the mackintosh is not the same as Joyce's or Woolf's, except in the case of D. and Rowe.

the dying refugee into a dark, drafty shed, where she maintains a vigil over him through the long cold night.

Toward morning when Coral discovers that Dr. Czinner is dead, she screams. Her scream does not go unheard; it reveals her hiding place. She stumbles out of the shed and through a group of soldiers into the arms of the waiting Mabel Warren, who whisks her into a car returning to Vienna. Mabel has boarded the Orient Express at Cologne after recognizing Dr. Czinner and sensing a news story. When he gives her the slip at Vienna, she follows him by car, catching up with him only in death at Subotica. While on the train Mabel has cultivated Coral, coveting her as a new companion. So the sequence of events in the shed at Subotica is all to Mabel's liking. She has an exclusive front-page story for the London *Clarion,* and she has Coral. " 'It's my story,' she claims with pride, allowing somewhere at the back of her mind, behind the headlines and the leaded type, a dream to form of Coral in pyjamas pouring out coffee, Coral in pyjamas mixing a cocktail, Coral asleep in the redecorated and rejuvenated flat."

When Coral first learns that Dr. Czinner is a Communist, she thinks of him momentarily "as one of the untidy men who paraded on Saturday afternoons in Trafalgar Square bearing hideous banners: 'Workers of the World, Unite,' 'Walthamstow Old Comrades,' 'Balham Branch of the Juvenile Workers' League.' They were the killjoys, who would hang the rich and close the theatres and drive her into dismal free love at a summer camp, and afterwards make her walk in procession down Oxford Street, carrying her baby behind a banner: 'British Women Workers.' " Later she admires him. If, at this point, Coral is a spokesman for the author (and it is not unreasonable to assume she is, since Greene is a critic of communism—*The Power and the Glory,* for example), then George Woodcock is justified in saying of Greene that "he has never let his just dislike of Marxist ideas and practice lead him into hatred of individual Communists."[22] To each his due is Greene's practice in the depiction of Communists. While Dr. Czinner and the police lieutenant in *The Power and the Glory* fight not for "new territory but a new world," Mr. Surrogate, the highbrow economist in *It's a Battlefield*, uses the party for his own self-aggrandizement.

As expressed in his fiction, Greene's political position is largely negative—anti-communistic and anti-capitalistic. (His strongest indictment of capitalism is to be found in *This Gun for Hire*.) But his animosity towards capitalism has not provoked him to portray all capitalists in an unfavorable light any more than he withholds sympathy from all his communistic characters. His capitalists are as different as Sir Marcus (*This Gun for Hire*), a caricature of a "robber baron," and Herbert Dreuther (*Loser Takes All*), a likable benefactor of the arts, with engaging foibles.

Often overcome by nostalgia for the Catholicism of his boyhood, Dr. Czinner secretly longs to return to the Church, to make a good confession. "The priest's face turned away, the raised fingers, the whisper of a dead tongue, seemed to him suddenly as beautiful, as infinitely desirable . . . as youth and first love in the corner of the viaduct wall." This is not very different from the equally irrepressible religious instinct of Minty, Anglican Minty, of whom Greene says, "a church claimed him. The darkness, the glow of the sanctuary lamp, drew him more than food. It was Lutheran, of course, but it had the genuine air of plaster images, of ever-burning light, of sins forgiven. He looked this way and that, he bent his head

[22] *The Writer and Politics*, p. 125.

and dived for the green door, with the caution and the dry-mouthed excitement of a secret debauchee."

Greene's business men are more successful in business transactions than in human relations. Myatt likes "being . . . with figures, with something that he could understand and that had no feelings." It is the same with tycoon Eric Krogh, who also "thinks in figures" and "doesn't feel vague things about people." In another respect Krogh resembles another passenger on the Orient Express, the best-selling novelist, Quin Savory. They both have risen from humble beginnings to exalted positions. Krogh has surmounted a peasant's birth; Savory, a bargain counter. But never losing their awareness of the grubby past, they are afraid of slips in manner that will betray them. They feel insecure, suffer from an inferiority complex, and continue to be surprised when other people accept them on equal terms.

The foreground characters in an entertainment usually have more background characters to compete with than is the case in a novel. For this reason the foreground characters in the entertainments are not so many-sided as their brethren in the novels. Yet the wonder is that Greene is able to provide as much information about their backgrounds and lives and individualize them as expertly as he does. The fact that he has a good ear for dialogue enables him to catch the reader's interest immediately. His lines have the honest ring of real talk. He knows, too, the little turns of speech by which people betray the texture of their souls. Witness Mabel Warren's interview with Quin Savory on the Orient Express. Sitting opposite him, noting his remarks, she reflects on how she hates success, represented in his case by "the sale of a hundred thousand copies," and loves failure, represented by other men she has interviewed, men "in prison cells, in hotel lounges, in mean back parlours." When Mabel asks Mr. Savory's opinion of modern literature—"'Joyce, Lawrence, all that?'"—he replies, "promptly with the effect of an epigram, 'It will pass.'"

III

Characteristic of Greene's technique in the entertainments is the ability to arrest the reader's attention immediately, the use of afterworld and underworld imagery, and the infiltration of autobiographical material:

Murder didn't mean much to Raven. It was just a new job. You had to be careful. You had to use your brains. It was not a question of hatred. He had seen the minister only once: he had been pointed out to Raven as he walked down the new housing estate between the little lit Christmas trees—an old, rather grubby man without any friends, who was said to love humanity.

The cold wind cut his face in the wide Continental street. It was a good excuse for turning the collar of his coat well up above his mouth. A harelip was a serious handicap in his profession. It had been badly sewn in infancy, so that now the upper lip was twisted and scarred. When you carried about you so easy an identification you couldn't help becoming ruthless in your methods. It had always, from the first, been necessary for Raven to eliminate the evidence.

These are the two opening paragraphs of *This Gun for Hire*. They immediately bring the reader, without meaningless meandering, into the world which he is to inhabit temporarily. The first sentence alone does this. The remainder of the first two paragraphs powerfully etches the portrait of Raven, a portrait etched in acid of a man alone, condemned to merciless ways by a harelip. Such a beginning is standard for Greene: all his tales take off well. The opening sentence of *Brighton*

Rock—"Hale knew, before he had been in Brighton three hours, that they meant to murder him"—further instances this. It creates at once the atmosphere of violence which is to envelop the story. *This Gun for Hire* also has a characteristic Greene ending. The circle is closed by visiting the characters in succession and discovering them in some typical situation. The violence that Raven metes out in the beginning is meted out to him at the close. Greene's stories make a full circle.

Greene's ability to open impressively is a trait he shares with some of the world's foremost novelists. Not the least memorable part of *Vanity Fair*, for instance, is the beginning, where the theme and the satirical tone emerge at once. Further examples of brilliant openings are these: the first three words of *Moby Dick*, "Call me Ishmael," with their stark Biblical overtone; the first sentence of *Anna Karenina*—"Happy families are all alike; every unhappy family is unhappy in its own way" —with its hint of the novel's psychological theme; the first three paragraphs of *Jane Eyre* with their dramatic contrast between the unloved child Jane and the contented, happy scene upon which she is looking; the first page of *Ulysses* with its foreshadowing of Christian and possibly Freudian themes.

The imagery in Greene's opening paragraph is often highly prophetic of what is to come. "The gulls swept over Dover. They sailed out like flakes of the fog, and tacked back towards the hidden town, while the siren mourned with them; other ships replied, a whole wake lifted up their voices—for whose death? The ship moved at half-speed through the bitter autumn evening. It reminded D. of a hearse." The multiple images of death with which *The Confidential Agent* opens are in keeping with the violence—beatings, explosions, man hunts, and murders—to follow.

Occasionally Greene's imagery has an autobiographical basis. Arthur Rowe, for example, sometimes imagines himself an insect underneath a stone. The same figure is repeated under different circumstances when Rowe, a patient in the plush nursing home, visits the run-down sick bay for the first time. He is left with the impression that "it was like the underside of a stone: you turned up the bright polished nursing home and found beneath it this." This insect-under-the-stone image recurs in Greene's non-fiction. In a truncated essay—he calls it "a personal note"—he recalls the revenge he swore on a boy who had plagued him at school. "For many years when I thought back on that period, I found the desire for revenge alive like a creature under a stone. The only change was that I looked under the stone less and less often. I began to write, and the past lost some of its power—I wrote it out of me. But still every few years a scent, a stretch of wall, a book in a shelf, a name in a newspaper, would remind me to lift the stone and see the creature move its head toward the light."[23]

Rowe is like Greene in yet another respect. Rowe "was brought up on stories of Captain Scott writing his last letters home, Oates walking into the blizzard . . . Damien among the lepers," *The Little Duke*, by Charlotte Yonge, and African adventure yarns. His heroes were brave, pure, and truthful, and life was simple and grand. "None of the books of adventure one read as a boy had an unhappy ending and none of them was disturbed by a sense of pity for the beaten side." But when the experience of life contradicts all this and Rowe learns the trick of suffering, he gradually falls into the habit of pity. Rowe the man reads and rereads *The Old Curiosity Shop* and *David Copperfield* "not so much because he liked them as because he had read them as a child and they carried

[23] "The Revenge," *Commonweal*, January 14, 1955, pp. 403-404.

no adult memories." They are part of a campaign intended to help him "mislay the events of twenty years" and blunt the point of his pity on fictitious sufferings.

Considering the rift between life as it is portrayed by juvenile books and life as it is, Rowe complains, "It's as if one had been sent on a journey with the wrong map." In "The Lost Childhood" Greene repeats this analogy when he also assesses the influence his childhood readings had upon his own life, so that Rowe's reflection has an autobiographical overtone:

But in childhood all books are books of divination, telling us about the future, and like the fortune teller who sees a long journey in the cards or death by water they influence the future. I suppose that is why books excited us so much. What do we ever get nowadays from reading to equal the excitement and the revelation of those first fourteen years? Of course I should be interested to hear that a new novel by Mr. E. M. Forster was going to appear this spring, but I could never compare that mild expectation of civilized pleasure with the missed heartbeat, the appalled glee I felt when I found on a library shelf a novel by Rider Haggard, Percy Westerman, Captain Brereton or Stanley Weyman which I had not read before. No, it is in those early years that I would look for the crisis, the moment when life took a new slant in its journey towards death.[24]

Rowe's fondness in youth for books on African exploration reflects Greene's own boyhood passion for *King Solomon's Mines.*

IV

Since *Loser Takes All* (1955) is so wholly different from the other entertainments, it deserves independent treatment. It belongs near the end, because in the very act of contrasting

[24] *The Lost Childhood*, p. 13.

it with the others, by indirection at least, I will be summing up some of the points I made earlier.

Loser Takes All is only the second entertainment to be written in the first person. The first, *The Third Man* (1950), is told by Calloway, a Scotland Yard inspector assigned to military duty in occupied Vienna. Whenever stories are written in the first person special problems inherent in that literary convention arise. As Percy Lubbock points out in *The Craft of Fiction*, readers can adjust themselves to the embarrassing intimacy of a narrator's revelations and even to the fact that the narrator writes with far more literary skill than such a person could be expected to possess.[25] But when Calloway pre-empts the exclusive right of an omniscient narrator, twice transcribing Martins' dreams and several times recording his thoughts, then the adjustment is uncomfortable and the illusion of reality is endangered.

Loser Takes All, a more successful story than *The Third Man*, is also told in the first person. This time the chief character, Bertram, is the narrator. Greene does not nod with Bertram the way he did with Calloway. The later entertainment is free from lapses in point of view. Bertram, an accountant in a London firm, is stranded with Cary, his bride, in Monte Carlo on their honeymoon, because Dreuther, his boss, does not arrive to take them on his yacht as he promised. When they begin to run out of funds, Bertram perfects a system and wins at the tables. With his winnings he secures the controlling shares in the Dreuther company and plans to punish his boss for having forgotten him. Meanwhile, Cary, feeling neglected, leaves him. Her departure coincides with Dreuther's belated arrival. When Dreuther reunites the honeymooners, Bertram forgives him.

[25] *The Craft of Fiction* (New York, Scribner, 1921), ch. IX.

In a brief dedicatory letter, Greene justly calls *Loser Takes All* a "frivolity," but he does not so describe any of his previous entertainments. This is because *Loser Takes All* is very different from its predecessors—different in characterization, motivation, plot, theme, and tone. By comparison this little tale (it is only novella length) teems with gaiety, humor, and playfulness. The characters are neither miserable nor self-tortured. They are not prisoners of the past, cut off from innocence in childhood's dark corners. Unfrightened, largely cheerful, they are spurred on by an expectation of happiness. "Lots of people aren't happy. We are," Cary says to Bertram on the eve of their marriage. They are an obvious exception to the generalization made by such critics as W. Gore Allen, Francis X. Connolly, and Richard Vorhees to the effect that Greene's characters are joyless people.[26]

Greene abandons the use of the pursuit sequence in *Loser Takes All*. No one here pursues self-identity relentlessly, and no one overtly pursues anyone else. No one suffers from an inner conviction of betrayal, and no one pledges timeless loyalty. There are no scrupulous policemen or unscrupulous lawbreakers; no thin girls who offend against nothing except purity and no morbid gangsters who offend against everything except purity. There is no crisscross in intrigue, no cosmic collision of good and evil, no bowel-twisting violence, no shocking evidence of horror or catastrophe. If the reader excepts a few scattered references to the Bible, the Catholic Church, original sin, and theologians, there is no traffic with the spiritual. When Greene relaxes his concern for the super-

[26] W. Gore Allen, "The World of Graham Greene," *Irish Ecclesiastical Record*, January 1949, pp. 44-45; F. X. Connolly, "The Spiritual Adventures of Graham Greene," *Renascence*, I (Spring 1949), 20; Richard Vorhees, "The World of Graham Greene," *South Atlantic Quarterly*, July 1951, p. 389.

natural, he rejoices in what is naturally good, as illustrated by this description of Cary:

There are so many faces in streets and bars and buses and stores that remind one of Original Sin, so few that carry permanently the sign of Original Innocence. Cary's face was like that—she would always until old age look at the world with the eyes of a child. She was never bored: every day was a new day: even grief was eternal and every joy would last for ever. "Terrible" was her favourite adjective—it wasn't in her mouth a *cliché*—there *was* terror in her pleasures, her fears, her anxieties, her laughter—the terror of surprise, of seeing something for the first time. Most of us only see resemblances, every situation has been met before, but Cary saw only differences, like a wine-taster who can detect the most elusive flavour.

Where mathematics is concerned, Bertram is never bored either. Good at statistics, he is not "able to understand the lay-man's indifference to figures. The veriest fool vaguely appreciates the poetry of the solar system—'the army of the un-alterable law'—and yet he cannot see the stately march of the columns, certain figures moving upwards, crossing over, one digit running the whole length of every column, emerging, like some elaborate drill at the Trooping the Colour." Bertram appreciates the poetry of numbers. He is normal (he thinks his bride-to-be is beautiful); he is healthy (he is on edge with wanting Cary the night before they are married); he is roman-tic (he thinks it gay to arrive at his wedding in a horse-cab); and he longs for the bucolic (he smells the country, tree scents and flower scents, in a London street on a balmy spring after-noon). He is not seedy, nor suspicious of well-being, like D. and Rowe.

Elderly, eccentric Herbert Dreuther, known familiarly as the Gom (the Grand Old Man), is a new breed of industrialist in Greene's work. He is certainly not malevolence incarnate like Sir Marcus in *This Gun for Hire*, nor is he tormented by a suffocating sense of loneliness and isolation like Eric Krogh in *The Shipwrecked*. The Gom, who is an intellectual Sybarite and a dilettante, quotes Baudelaire's line, "*Luxe, calme et volupté*," with approval, mistrusts classicism, and collects Renoirs and Boudins. He is cultured, courteous, and fluent. He talks with easy familiarity to social inferiors and foreigners. "Whatever the man's language he would have spoken it perfectly—he was of the Pentecostal type." His is glib. He is never "foxed for an explanation," and he can sweep "his mistakes into limbo on a tide of words." Four times married, the Gom gives Ovidean counsel, delightful and wicked, on *affaires de coeur*. This elegant and indecent cynic can say (unintentionally parodying Bacon's wise man, that made answer to the question, when a man should marry): "If one must marry it is better to marry a bad woman." About adultery he is more optimistic: "So often one has discovered how much one loves by sleeping with another."

In his earlier entertainments and novels Greene, like Mauriac, displays a compulsive conscience, emphasizes the sordid side of life, and looking at human nature finds little that is naturally good. Greene's usual characters—tortured by evil and guilt—and their usual emotion—"fear in a handful of dust"—are similar to Dostoyevsky's. "But," as Richard Vorhees observes, "at this very point of resemblance the difference between the two novelists is revealed. In the midst of Dostoyevsky's morbidness there is healthiness, besides his pathological melancholy there is gaiety, along with the twisted and hideous emotions of his characters there is wholesome love. But in Greene there is little or none of these positive qualities. Like Lear, he needs an ounce of civet to sweeten his imagination."[27]

[27] Vorhees, *op. cit.*, p. 395.

The aforementioned positive qualities, "healthiness," "gaiety," and "wholesome love," surface for the first time in *Loser Takes All*. The tone of the book is undeniably calmer, more normal, and more cheerful than was usual with Greene.

v

Apparently *Loser Takes All* was the ounce of civet Greene needed, for it was followed by *Our Man in Havana* (1958). With its lack of special emphasis on sin and neurosis and its light touch, the latter is the one entertainment of Greene's that resembles the novels of Evelyn Waugh. Here Greene displays, for the first time, a talent Waugh was born with — the ability to look into a mirror and make faces at himself. By turning the engrossing nightmare thrillers of the nineteen thirties and nineteen forties inside out, Greene lampoons the very type of spy-adventure story that he did so much to popularize.

Mixing mirth and murder, pomposity and poison, satire and suspense, Greene declares "waugh" in *Our Man in Havana*. He directs a contemptuous attack against bureaucracy in the British Secret Service and against hypocrisy in international relations. The central character is one Jim Wormold, the Havana representative of Phastkleaners, Ltd., an English vacuum-cleaner firm. His habit of treating consequential matters—like killing a man deliberately—inconsequentially seems to be right out of the pages of *A Handful of Dust*. And his decoration at the end, an Order of the British Empire, seeming to come right out of the pages of *Scoop*, constitutes putting out more flags.

From the opening pages, when Wormold is reluctantly recruited by the Secret Service in the gentlemen's washroom at Sloppy Joe's, it is clear that a burlesque of the cloak-and-dagger business is in the making. As agent 59200/5, Wormold is expected to uncover Cuban-based plots against British hold-ings in the Caribbean, even though he is totally ignorant of espionage and is temperamentally ill-suited for the work. The fun thereafter is supplied by his frantic efforts to live up to his assignment. He invents various sub-agents, some fictitious, some real—their names having been chosen at random from the telephone directory—in whose name he draws expenses and on whose "word" he concocts lurid reports of enemy mis-siles so potentially destructive as to render the hydrogen bomb obsolete. Accompanying his reports are "drawings" of this new weapon: magnified sketches of the Atomic Pile Suction Cleaner, Phastkleaner's latest two-way-action model.

Beguiled into thinking him a dangerous man, the enemy—whose nationality is never defined—marks Wormold for assassination. But an attempted poisoning at a business luncheon is thwarted by as enticing and artful a dodge as parody can contrive. When a dachshund wanders into the dining room, laps up the whisky Wormold spills, dies, and thus gives warn-ing of poison, even the most spoof-proof reader rejoices in the whole huge lark.

The spirit of parody is even served by the ironic ending. His deception on the edge of being exposed, the Man in Havana resigns his post and flies to London to abandon himself to the mercy of his employers. They have little choice. Far more con-cerned for the security of their jobs than the security of their country, and unwilling to confess publicly that they have been hoodwinked, Wormold's superiors recommend him for a decoration and give him a new assignment. "We thought the best thing for you under the circumstances would be to stay at home—on our training staff. Lecturing. How to run a station abroad. That kind of thing."

Our Man in Havana introduces a new and lighter shade of

"greene," becoming to the funny bone. Rather than repeat the same shade that was becoming to gooseflesh in all his previous full-length entertainments, Greene experiments. I take the experiment to be a successful one. The willingness to change a sure-fire formula for producing slick, cliff-hanging spy thrillers for an untried, uncertain one is a sign of Greene's moral courage. His success is a sign of his literary adaptability.

All of Greene's entertainments, and most of his novels, have been turned into motion pictures. Naturally some of these films have been more successful than others. Those such as *Orient Express, The Power and the Glory,* and *The End of the Affair,* in which the screen play was written by someone other than Greene, have been least successful. Greene has described his disappointment in seeing the film made from *Orient Express.* "It had been an instructive and rather painful experience to see it shown. The direction was incompetent, the photography undistinguished, the story sentimental. If there was any truth in the original it had been carefully altered; if anything was left unchanged it was because it was untrue."[28] The films—*The Fallen Idol* and *The Third Man*—in which Greene teamed with director Carol Reed have been most successful. The film adapted from *Our Man in Havana* is the third one made by this combination. Like their previous collaborations, this one is characterized by a sprightly screen play and the ingenious use of atmosphere, musical as well as visual,[29] so integrated with the story as to enhance not only the events but also the characterization. Reed "used the Hermanos Deniz Cuban Rhythm Band to play the background score and, like every other element, it contributes to and supports the over-all

[28] *Journey Without Maps*, p. 19.
[29] *The Third Man* combined distinguished photography with a memorable zither theme song.

effect of excitement and tension. Even the Cuban strippers seen through the smoky air of Havana night clubs or in revealing close-ups do not distract but add to the atmosphere and serve as ironic contrast to the muddled conspiracies that wind and unwind in the foreground."[30]

In some ways, the motion picture is an improvement on the book; in at least one way, it is not. The cast, uniformly excellent, is led by Alec Guinness as the Havana con man and includes Noël Coward as the secret agent who recruits him, Ralph Richardson as the top man in London, Burl Ives as the German doctor, Ernie Kovacs as the captain of police, and Maureen O'Hara as the secretary. In at least two places, the movie spikes the comedy with additional farce. When Coward, in the washroom confrontation scene with Guinness, forgets the umbrella he habitually carries, the stereotyped spy with his meticulous attention is travestied. The picture introduces another happy spree of whimsey in the rendezvous scene at Kingston where Coward warns Guinness that the enemy plans to murder him. Coward ribs the preposterous precautions taken by the stereotyped spy to prevent his conversation from being overheard by cautiously closing a flimsy *slatless* bamboo frame garden gate just prior to his admonition. A less felicitous change introduced into the screen play involves the death of the liquor-lapping dachshund. The dog is so much the object of sympathy in the picture that satire melts into sentimentality at this point. (In the book the satirical spirit is sustained here by a series of ludicrous similes.) In any case, both the book and the movie have enough comic shot and shell to splinter the most formidable funny bone.

[30] Paul Beckley, reviewing *Our Man in Havana* in the *New York Herald Tribune*, January 28, 1960.

4 The Catholic Novels

Brighton Rock (1938) is the first of five consecutive novels of Graham Greene that deserve to be treated together by reason of a common concern. The remaining four are *The Power and the Glory* (1940), *The Heart of the Matter* (1948), *The End of the Affair* (1951), and *The Quiet American* (1956). The overt inclusion of Roman Catholic doctrine is the fundamental difference between the earlier novels and these middle-period productions. In the latter, most of the chief characters are Catholics, and Catholicism is an essential element of the plot. God and Satan, virtue and sin, openly concern the characters. Pinkie, the Priest, Scobie, and Sarah are preoccupied with the issue of salvation and damnation. They are torn between the fatal attraction of evil and the redemptive power of grace. None of this is exclusively Catholic, but the fact that they are conditioned by their reception of the sacraments is, of course. Introspecting his enormous inclination to evil, Pinkie boasts: "Perhaps when they christened me, the holy water didn't take. I never howled the devil out."

Dramatizing theological problems, Greene presents a religious view of life. Although these novels are explicitly Catholic, they are in no sense narrow, cozy, complacent, or moralistic. They are Catholic without being aggressively sectarian, highly denominationalized, or piously evangelical. They confirm Greene's statement, in the preface to a book about him by the

French critic Paul Rostenne,[1] that he has no *a priori* edifying
intention in writing his novels but is simply driven by the
destiny of his characters. Rather than edifying, Greene troubles us. By presenting the mystery of suffering people, thus
inviting the reader to meditate on his own destiny, he fulfills
the function of the Christian novelist. With the publication of
Brighton Rock, he steadfastly started to explore the central
drama: the human soul engaged in its adventure with eternity.
Greene is a man set on earth to explore the labyrinthine ways.

Brilliant as *It's a Battlefield* and *The Shipwrecked* are, there
is a considerable difference in achievement between them and
the more recent novels. For while the theme of flight and
pursuit remains the same, the characters are now presented
sub specie aeternitatis. Pursuer and pursued are ideological and
spiritual foes, representatives of opposing orders. They are
the "cold" (Pinkie and the Lieutenant of police), the "hot"
(the Priest and Sarah), and the "lukewarm" of Apocalypse iii,
14-16 (Ida). In the Catholic novels, worlds collide: the world
that ignores Christ with the one in which invisible realities are
the supreme ones; the world that denies any efficacy to human
suffering with the one that envisions suffering as the desidera-
tum for beatification; the world that effaces the traces of original sin with the world that painstakingly retraces original sin;
the world where love is actuated solely by egotistic impulses
with the world where love is the final answer to evil; and the
world that sees no sin where there is sin with the world that is
not sin-blind.

The characters in the pre-Catholic novels show awareness
of their neuroses; the characters in the Catholic novels show
awareness of their sins as well. This marriage of Catholicism

[1] *Graham Greene: témoin des temps tragiques* (Paris, Juillard,
1949), p. 11.

and abnormal psychology raises a problem concerning the ultimate freedom of Greene's characters. Is Pinkie predestined to hell? Or does he deliberately damn himself? These questions can be asked of all Greene's heroes and heroines; they do not apply solely to the boy gangster. Many French critics—among them Jean Duché, Claude-Edmonde Magny, and Jean-H. Roy —feel that Greene presents his characters as prisoners and God as the jailer.[2] But it is highly improbable, as William Birmingham observes, that "the function of religion in Greene's novels is to imprison his heroes and give them only the merit of perceiving man's tragic situation."[3] There is far more evidence in Greene's novels for the counter-notion: none of his characters is a hostage of fatality. Paul Rostenne convincingly shows that Greene's sinners are not unalterably controlled by fate; they are merely liable to it.[4] By co-operating with the liberating power of grace, as the Priest and Sarah do, they can escape this subjection. Even Pinkie, who rejects God's grace and so fails to side-step fate, progresses from captivity to sin to a point where virtue is at least a critical temptation.

The presentation of pity is more involved in the later novels. In the pre-Catholic novels, the most sympathetic characters, Andrews and Conrad, are motivated by pity; in the Catholic novels, the least sympathetic (with the obvious exception of Scobie), Ida and the Lieutenant, are motivated by pity. Pity is based on opposition to pain in the sympathetic and unsympa-

[2] Jean Duché, "Du Rocher de Sysyphe au Rocher de Brighton," *La Table ronde*, II (1948), 308; Claude-Edmonde Magny, "Graham Greene," *Poésie*, XXXII (1946), 35; Jean-H. Roy, "L'Oeuvre de Graham Greene ou un christianisme de la damnation," *Les Temps modernes*, LII (1950), 1518.

[3] "Graham Greene Criticism: A Bibliographical Study," *Thought*, XXVII (Spring 1952), 81.

[4] Rostenne, *op. cit.*, p. 85.

thetic alike. Andrews' pursuit of self-identity is so painful that it causes him to wallow in self-pity. Conrad's frenzied desire to arrest the suffering of his brother and sister-in-law springs from his pity for them. Pity accompanies Ida's hedonism and the Lieutenant's communism. It is their only weapon, their sole ethic, in the all-out war they wage to annihilate pain. In *Brighton Rock*, it is Ida, not Rose, who is ruled by pity; in *The Power and the Glory*, it is the Lieutenant, not the Priest, who is ruled by pity. Those who pity in the Catholic novels exist in a separate universe of belief from those who do not. Pity is the ethic of those who try to substitute themselves for God. Only in the person of Scobie does Greene endeavor to delineate pity in a character committed to a higher moral order. But the deeds that pity inspires in Scobie are ultimately attempts "to dispense with God, to wrestle with God,"[5] so that the shadow of the Lieutenant lies over him.

Greene's grasp of technique is more certain in the Catholic novels. From the first Greene displayed the ability to set a scene deftly and economically, but he has steadily improved with regard to the evocation of place. Stockholm, the site of international financial intrigue in *The Shipwrecked*, is summoned up satisfactorily but with nothing like the skill that is lavished on Freetown, the locale of wartime political intrigue in *The Heart of the Matter*. Krogh's downfall could conceivably have occurred elsewhere, not so Scobie's downfall. No cloudy corners, no uncertain recesses, mar the evocation of Freetown. Fact is not added laboriously to fact so that the place description consists of a mere mechanical sum of details, but care is taken to integrate suggestive indications of background with psychological developments. So masterfully is

⁵ Raymond Jouve, "La Damnation de Scobie?" *Etudes*, November 1949, p. 177.

the sense of place woven into *The Heart of the Matter* that the continuous oppressive heat and the ever-present carrion birds, more ominous in the later stages of the book, naturally symbolize the increasing failures and impending death of Scobie. Greene even pictures Scobie's way of life by describing inanimate things. The rusty handcuffs that hang in Scobie's office, for example, symbolize his inability to apply the law to the crafty natives who constantly circumvent it by endless evasions and lies.

Often overlooked is the fact that the heroines of Greene's Catholic novels are occasions of grace as well as comfort. *Brighton Rock*'s Rose, for example, is thin, plain, and, like Lucia, not at all chic. She commits sins of the flesh without much desire, like Milly. She has spent a life among the guilty without being corrupted, like Elizabeth. This has led W. Gore Allen to charge that the heroines of Greene's novels are all alike.[6] But the dissimilarity between the girls in the pre-Catholic novels and the girls in the Catholic novels is more important than the similarities. Caught up in some dark theology, Rose is an overt instrument of God's grace, whereas Elizabeth is not even explicitly religious, although she is the voice of love. Elizabeth loves Andrews to her utmost capacity, which is considerable, and yet it would never have occurred to her —as it does to Rose after failing to save Pinkie—to express sincere willingness to forgo salvation in order to be damned with her lover. The intrusion of the supernatural, in the form of the communion of saints and "the communion of sinners," is the difference between the pre-Catholic and the Catholic heroine.

[6] W. Gore Allen, *op. cit.*, p. 44.

11

Greene's leading characters fall into two classes. There are those like Pinkie and Major Scobie who really never learn anything in this life. And then there are those like the Priest and Sarah Miles who finally come to understand that the only thing on earth worse than not getting your own way is getting your own way.

Brighton Rock is a form of stick candy. Break it anywhere and the word "Brighton" appears on the ends of the stick. The seventeen-year-old gangster, Pinkie Brown, is like Brighton Rock: he is boundaried by the word "evil." But he needs to be coupled to goodness. "She was good," he concludes with respect to the innocent adolescent waitress, Rose Wilson, "and he was damned: they were made for each other." The core of *Brighton Rock* is not only Pinkie's knowledge of how he and Rose complement each other but also his knowledge of how they differ from their relentless pursuer, Ida Arnold. "She [Ida] was as far from either of them as she was from Hell—or Heaven. Good and evil lived in the same country, spoke the same language, came together like old friends, feeling the same completion. . . ." Living in the secular country of right and wrong, Ida cannot comprehend why Rose loves Pinkie. Believing in neither heaven nor hell, she does not understand that in their eyes "the world never moved: it lay there always the ravaged and disputed territory between the two eternities. They faced each other as it were from opposing territories, but like troops at Christmas time they fraternized." So Ida, the self-appointed guardian of justice, who "had no pity for something she didn't understand," becomes preoccupied with saving Rose and punishing Pinkie.

Cheery, fun-loving Ida, the big-breasted personification of boozy good times and of light-hearted coition that has about the same moral value as a blowout on stout and oysters, hunts Pinkie with booming laughter and risqué songs. With an erroneous conscience, she has no sense of her own sinfulness. Morally unconscious, Ida is a sort of female Tom Jones, considering herself imprudent at times but never sinful. In place of the moral law, she substitutes a cult of fair play which condones adultery—"It did no one any harm, it was just human nature"—and ignores God but draws the line at murder. "Death shocked her, life was so important. She wasn't religious. She didn't believe in heaven or hell, only in ghosts, ouija boards, tables that rapped and little inept voices speaking plaintively of flowers. Let Papists treat death with flippancy: life wasn't so important perhaps to them as what came after; but to her death was the end of everything." Ida is the direct antithesis of Rose and Pinkie. Her credo is "camaraderie, good nature, cheeriness . . . justice, an eye for an eye, law and order, capital punishment, a bit of fun now and then . . . nothing mysterious." She is nowhere a stranger in the world; she lives by platitudes and sucks the mystery out of life; she is jolly and hearty, blowsy and vital. Belonging to the great law-abiding middle class, Ida epitomizes the sensual warmth of the body and the absence of faith.

There are two kinds of people to be found in Brighton, and by implication in the world: those like Pinkie and Rose and those like Ida. Ida's kinsfolk comprise the vast majority. They even include the members of Pinkie's gang: Dallow, who boasts, "I don't believe in what my eyes don't see"; Spicer, who has no fear of God, only of the police; Cubbitt, who covers up his sad romantic feelings with an air of coarse joviality. Colleoni, the prosperous leader of the rival gang, is the char-

acter most like Ida. The visible world is all his: "the cash
registers and policemen and prostitutes, Parliament and the
laws which say 'this is Right and this is Wrong.' " In Brighton,
at least, Pinkie and Rose are virtually solitaries. They feel
themselves strangers in the bright and lustful world of Ida and
Colleoni. Only the darkness is native to them. Hale, the slain
newspaper man, and Drewitt, the cracked old lawyer given
to literary phrases and thoughts of indecent exposure, in a
small way share Pinkie and Rose's knowledge of another,
darker world. When Hale is desperately trying to elude
Pinkie's gang, he recalls how "from childhood he had loved
secrecy, a hiding place, the dark." When Drewitt reflects on
his unfortunate marriage, he is reminded of what Mephi-
stopheles replied to Faustus when he asked where hell was.
"He said: 'Why, this is hell, nor are we out of it.' "

Dante merely visited hell; Pinkie comes from there. His
short life—like that of Rimbaud—is spent on the side of hell,
enlisted in the cause of the Prince of Darkness. By exploiting
her blind devotion to him, Pinkie tempts Rose to kill herself.
This figure of pure malevolence only pretends to love her,
all the time actually hating her, so that he may obtain her
willed consent to a sham suicide pact that will insure his temporal safety in return for her immortality of pain. Even though
unsuccessful, this maneuver is the crowning achievement in
his satanic career. Pinkie's maturation as an agent of evil is as
gradual as a saint's progression in goodness. Contemplating his
forthcoming fraudulent marriage to Rose and the state of
mortal sin into which it will plunge them, Pinkie is filled with
awe at his diabolical devolution in evil. "He had graduated in
pain: first the school dividers had been left behind, next the
razor. He had a sense now that the murders of Hale and Spicer
were trivial acts, a boy's game, and he had put away childish

things. Murder had only led to this—this corruption." The practice of torments with dividers split open a chink on the rim of the universe so that Pinkie could glimpse the evil that was yet to erupt.

Pinkie's rebellion against God calls to mind the words of T. S. Eliot in an essay on Baudelaire:

So far as we are human, what we do must be either evil or good; so far as we do evil or good, we are human; and it is better, in a paradoxical way, to do evil than to do nothing: at least, we exist. It is true to say that the glory of man is his capacity for salvation; it is also true to say that his glory is his capacity for damnation. The worst that can be said of most of our malefactors, from statesmen to thieves, is that they are not men enough to be damned.[7]

The worst cannot be said of Pinkie: he is at least man enough to be damned. Like Baudelaire, he has looked the devil straight in the face and revels perversely in his capacity for damnation. "Credo in unum Satanum," he mockingly blasphemes. "The Boy couldn't picture any eternity except in terms of pain." Even his features attest to his affinity with the lower depths: "the slaty eyes were touched with the annihilating eternity from which he had come and to which he went." Whenever this monster of labyrinthine wickedness brushes against goodness—his early religious experience or the childlike faith of Rose, for example—he feels compelled to soil or pervert it. Only once does the spectacle of goodness stagger him. Walking down an alley, the Boy sees an old woman sitting upon the ground. "He could just see the rotting and discoloured face: it was like the sight of damnation. Then he heard the whisper: 'Blessed art thou among women,' saw the grey

[7] "Baudelaire," *Selected Essays* (New York, Harcourt, 1932), p. 344.

fingers fumbling at the beads. This was not one of the damned; he watched with horrified fascination: this was one of the saved."

"The greatest saints," Greene has written in an essay on the demoniac Frederick Rolfe, "have been men with more than a normal capacity for evil, and the most vicious men have sometimes narrowly evaded sanctity."[8] To make Pinkie a fictional counterpart of Rolfe, the self-styled Baron Corvo, was never Greene's intention, and yet the similarities are amazing. Pinkie is a great sinner who might have become a great saint, just as Rolfe was a potential saint who took the wrong turn. As a child, Pinkie swore he would be a priest. Rolfe, too, was a spoiled priest. "He would be a priest or nothing . . . if he could not have Heaven, he would have Hell."[9] His devilish pride "would not accept even Heaven, except on his own terms."[10] With Pinkie, it is no different: "Heaven was a word; Hell was something he could trust." Pinkie's unwanted sexuality is akin to Rolfe's detestation of the flesh. Rolfe was lost through an excess of faith unaccompanied by hope and charity. For the same lack of hope and charity, Pinkie is perverted to evil. Rolfe's pilgrimages to the rim of the Inferno find their equivalent in the Boy's habit of regarding his room at Billy's as hell. Like Rolfe, Pinkie succumbs to temptation on the grand scale and stoops to vice of a kind that can only be deemed satanic.

Pinkie is a psychologically impotent young man who finds sexual release and relief from the horror inside him in the practice of torments. His repressed sexuality is perverted into sadism. His nearest approach to passion consists in inflicting pain with nails, splinters, razor blades, and school dividers. He

[8] *The Lost Childhood*, p. 93.
[9] *Ibid.*, p. 94.
[10] *Ibid.*, p. 93.

longs to tear a strip of sticking plaster from Spicer's cheek, to see the skin break, and instead of kissing Rose, he longs "to strike her, to make her scream." The little sensual rages he displays by dismembering a leather jacket or crushing a moth under his shoe further instance his cruelty and recall the way Minty derived pleasure from imprisoning a spider under an upturned glass. The Boy's abstention from liquor, chocolates, cigarettes, dancing, gambling, and girls is an escape from the sexual encounters he was forced to witness as a child and a sign that he is afraid to get entangled with life. Through "a kind of hideous and unnatural pride," he shrinks from the sexual act. He feels no desire, and he would never have given himself up to marriage—"To marry: it was like ordure on the hands"—were there any other way to guarantee his immunity from the law. By attempting intercourse with Sylvie, Spicer's girl, Pinkie shores himself up against his wedding night. But his effort to acquire the habit of a woman is such a disagreeable failure that he retches and declares he would rather hang than marry. Thus, a mere two nights later, when he consummates a painful copulation with Rose, it seems as though his psychological block is overcome too easily.

Pinkie is Greene's most Dostoyevskean character. Like several characters in *The Possessed*, he revolts dramatically against God and is obsessed with suicide. Pinkie is a blend of Stavrogin, the suicide who tortures children, Kirillov, the suicide who quarrels with God, and Pyotr Stepanovitch, the murderer who kills for pleasure. The Boy, like Raskolnikov in *Crime and Punishment*, is the protagonist in a supernatural "cops and robbers" story. The murder of Hale parallels Raskolnikov's murder of the old pawnbroker. Napoleonic dreams of grandeur motivate both of them: Pinkie desires to usurp Colleoni's empire; Raskolnikov wants to prove himself exempt from the natural law. But their plans go astray: their crimes lead not to emancipation but to isolation. Their increasing alienation from life is arrested by two self-sacrificing girls to whom they turn unwillingly. Sonia, the prototype of Rose—even to offending against purity without much pleasure—and Rose are the light-bearers who offer regeneration to these sons of darkness. More-over what Pinkie owes to Freud—his hatred, his desire for castration, his utter disregard for human life, his guilt and anxiety—is ultimately a debt to Dostoyevsky, that daring proto-cartographer of the country of psychoanalysis, whom Freud himself acknowledged as one of his masters.

The nameless priest in *The Power and the Glory* is the object of two pursuits—human and divine. The human pursuit is relentlessly conducted by a nameless lieutenant of police in the state of Tabasco in Southern Mexico during the Commu-nist persecution of the Catholic Church in the nineteen thirties. The pursued is the one remaining Catholic priest in the prov-ince, who tries desperately to avoid being taken by the Red Shirts in order to carry on his humble ministrations among the people, many of whom remain stubbornly loyal to the faith. On this natural level, the Priest is both an outlaw and a scape-goat. In a double sense, he is an outlaw: according to the laws of the new godless state, the Priest is an outlaw merely because he persists in his sacred duties; but he has also defied some of the laws of the Church. Linking the natural to the super-natural level, the portrait of the Priest as a scapegoat is more subtle. Starved, driven from village to village, the fugitive continues being a priest to his people until his final betrayal and capture, whereupon he undergoes something of the Passion of Christ, the supreme scapegoat. With the divine pursuit, the drama becomes metaphysical. Obviously, the pursuit by God cannot be pictured, but from the Priest's thoughts, words, and actions we infer the transformation of Tabasco "into the whole wasteland of original sin, the Priest into the human soul and the flight from the police into the flight of the soul from God."[11] This sinful priest is ultimately pursued by the Hound of Heaven down the labyrinthine ways to his own salvation.[12]

The salvation offered by the Priest, the representative of Christ, conflicts with the salvation offered by the Lieutenant, the representative of Caesar. The Priest is skeptical of beatitude on earth. He urges his people to practice self-denial if they wish one day to become citizens of heaven. Furthermore, his own life illustrates the precept that the journey to joy must pass through the desert of pain. Fanatically opposed to what he considers pie-in-the-sky pipe dreams, the Lieutenant works tirelessly for an earthly Utopia. Social revolution and materialistic progress, to the exclusion of prayer and spiritual progress, are his blueprint for a better world. He recalls another Marxist character of Greene's, Dr. Czinner, who loves the poor and tells himself "that God was a fiction invented by the rich to keep the poor content." Fighting for children, the Lieutenant "would eliminate from their childhood everything which had made him miserable, all that was poor, superstitious and corrupt," but like so many of Greene's other policemen, he is helpless, unable to realize his ambition, because he has nothing but his own empty "certainty in the existence of a dying, cooling world of human beings who had evolved from animals for no purpose at all." Besides, his practice of shooting innocent

[11] James Newman, "The Divine Pursuit," *Juggler*, April 1947, p. 32. Newman was the first to point out that *The Power and the Glory* is an insight into the soul's relations with its Creator.

[12] This interpretation is re-enforced by the fact that when the novel first appeared in America, it was entitled *The Labyrinthine Ways*.

hostages is at sharp variance with the death sentence he imposes upon injustice, inequality, cruelty, misery, unhappiness, and pain.

The sinfulness of the Priest is in marked contrast with the exemplary personal life of the Lieutenant. The Priest is a drunkard and a fornicator. The Lieutenant is celibate, self-sacrificing, altruistic, and dedicated—all the things a priest ought to be. In all ways, save one, the Lieutenant is the better man: he is unable to help his countrymen; his love is without issue. Since Christ has not made the means of salvation to depend on the sanctity of His priests and He is willing to give grace to souls through sacraments administered even by sinful priests, the Priest is more fortunate: he is able to help his countrymen; his love is not sterile.[13] After his final arrest, this is the point the Priest tries to impress upon the Lieutenant:

"That's another difference between us. It's no good your working for your end unless you're a good man yourself. And there won't always be good men in your party. Then you'll have all the old starvation, beating, get-rich-anyhow. But it doesn't matter so much my being a coward—and all the rest. I can put God into a man's mouth just the same—and I can give him God's pardon. It wouldn't make any difference to that if every priest in the Church was like me."

Pinkie is a composite of the two antagonists in *The Power and the Glory*. In many ways, the Priest resembles Pinkie. They are pursued to the death by hostile ideologists. They carry hell about with them, and evil runs like malaria in their veins, as they wrestle with Satan. They quest for peace which,

[13] Catholic teaching dissociates the sacramental functions of the priest from his own spiritual condition, as having their validity *ex opere operato* not *ex opere operantis*.

as in the case of D. and Scobie, amounts to an escape from life, a death-wish. Fragments of remembered liturgy are constantly in their thoughts. Though their reaction is very different, they are frequently humiliated. By accepting humiliation, the Priest ascends to the sanctified heights of martyrdom; by rejecting humiliation, Pinkie descends to the Luciferean depths of wounded pride. The part played by humiliation in Greene's work is not unlike the part humiliation plays in the lives of Smerdyakov and Alyosha in *The Brothers Karamazov*. In many ways, the Lieutenant resembles Pinkie: they share a feeling of childhood betrayal, enmity with God, soured virginity, neurotic pride, an ascetic life, apostasy, and passion for destruction.

On the level of religious persecution, the Priest is the central figure in a thundering modern parable on the indestructibility of religious faith. When the Priest is captured and shot, the Lieutenant is the apparent victor in the tense struggle which has ensued between the two. But the victory is only apparent, for *The Power and the Glory* is less a story about a whisky priest than a dramatic enactment of the utilization of an imperfect human agent by God. God employs the execution of the Priest, which represents the very epitome of success for the foes of religion, to renew the faith of the boy Luis. The revival of religious sympathy in Luis—for whom the Lieutenant "was quite prepared to make a massacre . . . first the Church and then the foreigner and then the politician"—symbolizes communism's lack of appeal to the youth of Tabasco. And so it is fitting that the new priest, who arrives surreptitiously to carry on the sacerdotal work of his predecessor, should put his trust exclusively in Luis.

Since "there was something of a priest in his intent observant walk," in his ascetic room "as comfortless as . . . a monastic

cell," in his lack of sexual indulgence, and in his compassion
for the downtrodden, it is strange that "a natural hatred as
between dog and dog" should "stir in the lieutenant's bowels"
whenever he contemplates his prey. Sometimes people who are
very much in love come to resemble one another. Perhaps the
reverse is also true: it is as if in his single-minded hatred the
Lieutenant has become a little like the object of that hatred.
But there is nothing personal in his contempt for the Priest: it
is God he is really against. "It infuriated him to think that there
were still people in the state who believed in a loving and
merciful God." He unleashes his nihilistic hatred against the
Priest only because he is the representative of God. To the
Lieutenant, the Priest represents the Church which was so deficient in social justice as to deserve liquidation. He makes a
scapegoat of the Priest. Like the people of the Old Testament
who heaped their sins on the head of a goat and drove him off
into the wilderness, the Lieutenant blames the Priest, the sole
visible sign of Catholicism in the whole countryside, for
misery, poverty, and superstition.

The Priest also acts as a scapegoat for his people. Twice he
seeks safety; twice he is called back to administer the last rites
to the dying. There is no escape. "He was like the King of a
West African tribe, the slave of his people, who may not even
lie down in case the winds should fail." Lest God should cease
to exist "in all this space between the sea and the mountains,"
this brandy-bibber dare not stop baptizing, hearing confessions, and saying Mass—even at the risk of his death in mortal
sin. The Catholics of Tabasco need his sacramental powers to
loose their sins. "When he raised the Host," above a packing-
case altar while celebrating a furtive and forbidden Mass in
an unventilated hut, "he could imagine their faces lifted like
famished dogs."

Modern Catholic novelists often employ priests as scapegoats and outcasts. Most of the priests who are major characters in the novels of Georges Bernanos serve as scapegoats. Père Donissan, the clumsy young priest in *Sous le soleil de Satan*, absorbs the sin of Mouchette, the possessed girl, in order to ransom her, and also assumes and supports the crushing weight of the wrecked lives left in his confessional. In *Journal d'un curé de campagne*, the diarist, an unpopular young priest, penetrates far into the pain of his parish, heals the squire's wife, and finally dies from and for the sins of his parishioners. François Mauriac,[14] too, presents the priest as a scapegoat. The villagers in *Les Anges noirs* impute to the innocent Abbé Alain Forcas, a figure of derision, all their secret sins. Raising no protest, he patiently, in a spirit of Christian forbearance, takes all their sins upon himself. Greene's belief in "the appalling mysteries of love moving through a ravaged world"[15] finds its perfect illustration in the priestly scapegoat.

The Priest as scapegoat images the high priest, Christ. In imitation of Christ, whose sense of eternal responsibility for others was demonstrated on Calvary, this meek Mexican curate withdraws the claims of self. In enduring sacrificial suffering for others he becomes Christ-like. The events in *The Power and the Glory* preceding the execution of the Priest intentionally imitate the actions that led up to the crucifixion: the ignoble half-caste betrayer is a yellow-toothed Judas; the agony in the cell block, Gethsemane; the temptation to escape to Las Casas, the temptation of Christ in the desert; the solace

[14] Greene admires the work of both Mauriac and Bernanos. He devotes a whole essay to the former (an essay from which I shall have occasion to quote at the end of this chapter) but simply alludes to the latter as having a sense of evil comparable to Henry James' (*The Lost Childhood*, p. 43).

[15] *Another Mexico*, p. 3.

the Priest offers the dying Yankee murderer, the solace Christ offers the good thief; the Lieutenant's stronger desire to destroy the Priest than the Yankee murderer, the multitude's stronger desire to shed Christ's blood than Barabbas'; craven Padre José's refusal to shrive the Priest, the denial by Peter. Unimaginable glory pools around the Priest's death, because he dies not for the good and the beautiful but for the half-hearted and the corrupt, just as Christ died for all the depravity in the world. Thus the power and the glory of the Father bursts forth from the whisky priest with the bastard child.

The Priest's outlaw status and his scapegoat status stem from the fact that he is a priest. The salvation the outlaw priest offers the people is love and the death of the scapegoat priest is an act of love, but, since he is a man first of all, his own evolution in love is the story of man in the world. *The Power and the Glory* unfolds a divine pursuit as well as a human one. The pursuit conducted by the Lieutenant has not the universal implications to be found in the one conducted by God. Whereas the Priest is the object of the Lieutenant's search and the locale is Communist Mexico, the human soul is God's object and the locale is this world. The divine pursuit results in metaphysical alchemy: the place, the central character, and the central action are turned into symbols. Tabasco represents the world as it has existed since the fall of Adam: a place whose order has been shattered by original sin and a people, in consequence, whose wills have been weakened and inclined towards evil; the Priest represents the soul of Everyman; and the search for the Priest by the police represents God's search for the human soul. (The analogy limps to the extent that God's search is benign while the Lieutenant's is not.) By staging the soul's progress to God, Greene suggests the thesis most fundamental to a novelist—the nature of man's relation to his Creator.

For depicting the immensity of the trip the soul has to make on its journey to salvation, Tabasco is an ideal site. It is the wasteland of original sin in symbolic microcosm. The landscape is ravaged by "vultures moving in the sky like indigestion spots," by sharks and alligators looking after the carrion in the sea and the rivers, by snakes "hissing away like match-flames through the grass," by malaria-carrying mosquitoes, by beetles detonating against the walls, by rats and body lice, and by hordes of tiny, almost microscopic, smut-like scraps of life. In the tropical heat there is no end to life or death. The relentless rain and the remorseless sun take turns battering the squalid villages, forests, and swamps. The inhabitants of Tabasco are also miserable: the village children "with bellies swollen by worms," eating "dirt from the bank"; the British dentist with his inadequate implements and his collapsing sanity; the turncoat priest living with his wife in abjection and insecurity; the Priest's illegitimate child with the world in her heart at seven "like the small spot of decay in a fruit"; the hypochondriacal Mrs. Fellows with a neurotic fear of death and a hatred of the tropics; and the treacherous, hypocritical half-caste who is a self-confessed procurer and pervert. Home is a phrase used by these people "to mean four walls behind which one slept." In Tabasco, where grace is largely rejected and sin has the field pretty much to herself, there is no end to directionless violence and nightmarish horror.

Two incidents involving the Priest, the one in the hotel and the one that follows it in jail, are typical of the atmosphere of dereliction and nightmare—so reminiscent of Kafka—which hovers over *The Power and the Glory*. Halfway through the novel, the Priest goes in disguise to the capital and with all his remaining money purchases bootleg beverages from the Governor's cousin, whom he has to toast along with the Chief of

Police in a shabby hotel room. In near-agony, yet having to simulate cheerfulness, he watches his tormentors "as they sat on the bed talking, with nothing to do and nothing to believe and nowhere better to go," consuming all his wine—which he needs for Mass—and most of his brandy—which he needs for courage—while "words like 'mystery' and 'soul' and 'the source of life' came in over and over again." Soon after the Priest departs, he is picked up by the Red Shirts who, inadvertently discovering the bottle of brandy, arrest him. The prison cell he occupies is "very like the world: overcrowded with lust and crime and unhappy love: it stank to heaven; but he realized that after all it was possible to find peace there. . . ."

And so even in Tabasco the Priest discovers that abandonment and desolation are not quite everywhere. Not all the inhabitants are wretched or cowed by totalitarianism. Despite the fact that there is a price on the head of the Priest, neither his fellow prisoners nor the villagers betray him to the police. Often heroism and faith come from the most unexpected quarters. Coral Fellows, the bony thirteen-year-old English girl who lives with her irresponsible parents at the banana station, has, unlike the Priest's daughter, heroically resisted life's attempt to get at her. Brigida laughs at her father and mocks him; Coral protects the Priest at considerable risk to herself. She is not ancient in the knowledge of evil as is Brigida, for whom corruption has been almost a corollary of self-consciousness. On another occasion, the fleeing Priest stumbles upon an Indian cemetery—"an odd grove of crosses"—on a remote plateau:

They were the first Christian symbols he had seen for more than five years publicly exposed. . . . No priest could have been concerned in the strange rough group; it was the work of Indians and had nothing in common with the tidy vestments of the Mass and the elaborately worked out symbols of the liturgy. It was like a short cut to the dark and magical heart of the faith—to the night when the grave opened and the dead walked.

This passage prompted the only significant comment François Mauriac has made on Greene. "We feel it is that hidden presence of God in an atheistic world, that subterranean flowing of Grace which dazzles Graham Greene much more than the majestic façade which the temporal Church still erects above the peoples."[16]

The suffering of the soul without God is symbolized by the suffering of the Priest in flight. And the soul's surrender to Love is symbolized by the perfect act of contrition made by the Priest in prison awaiting execution:

Tears poured down his face: he was not at the moment afraid of damnation—even the fear of pain was in the background. He felt only an immense disappointment because he had to go to God empty-handed, with nothing done at all. It seemed to him at that moment that it would have been quite easy to have been a saint. It would only have needed a little self-restraint and a little courage. He felt like someone who has missed happiness by seconds at an appointed place. He knew now at the end that there was only one thing that counted—to be a saint.

As with the God-smitten Priest, snatched up by the Communion of Saints and hoisted aloft to signal the Triumph of Divine Love, so it is with the soul pulled back from sin by the vast stretch of God's Love. From the story of this bibulous priest we learn that the results of original sin and the signifi-

[16] "Graham Greene," *Men I Hold Great* (New York, Philosophical Library, 1951), p. 126.

cance of love are the universal elements in any relationship of man to God.

There is yet no agreement on who or what Major Scobie, in *The Heart of the Matter*, is. Critical estimates of his character have run the gamut. No character of Greene's has received such extremes of interpretation as Scobie. In judgments which mock consistency we hear him called a saint and a murderer, a self-sacrificing Catholic and a bad Catholic—in fact almost any pair of contraries that can be imagined.[17]

Before we can understand Scobie, we must ascertain Greene's intention in *The Heart of the Matter*. The epigraph —a quotation from Charles Péguy—is surely a clue: "Le pécheur est au coeur même de chrétienté. . . . Nul n'est aussi compétent que le pécheur en matière de chrétienté. Nul, si ce n'est le saint." Evidently then, Greene, in the character of

[17] For Marie Mesnet, in *Graham Greene and the Heart of the Matter*, one of Scobie's outstanding faults is his propensity to self-deception (p. 67); but Kenneth Allott, in *The Art of Graham Greene*, concludes that "from his responsibility and practical sense springs his inability to deceive himself" (p. 223). Henry M. Robinson, reviewing for *The Saturday Review* (July 10, 1948), says "the idea keeps recurring to me that Major Scobie is, in his obscure station, an all-suffering *alter Christus*" (p. 9); yet an anonymous reviewer for *Time* (August 9, 1948) says he is "a sinner disguised as a hero-villain" (p. 82). Another anonymous reviewer for *Newsweek* (July 12, 1948) believes Scobie to be "one of those rare creatures in life or fiction, a truly good man" (p. 85); whereas Dietrich von Hildebrand, in *True Morality and Its Counterfeits*, implies that he is a glorified sinner (p. 3). Evelyn Waugh, writing for *Commonweal* (July 16, 1948), is certain that Greene wants us to believe all Scobie's deeds are actuated by love of God (p. 324); while Jane Howes, writing for *The Catholic World* (April 1950), is equally certain that Greene meant to show the exact opposite in *The Heart of the Matter*: "a soul's complete degeneration" (p. 39).

Scobie, has tried to make plausible the paradox that "the sinner is at the very heart of Christendom." But does he succeed? Does *The Heart of the Matter* do justice to the idea? Is Scobie presented as extraordinarily competent "in the matter of Christendom"? To answer these questions let us pursue the method used by Percy Lubbock in *The Craft of Fiction* to determine the efficiency of novels. It is appropriate to apply Lubbock's procedure to *The Heart of the Matter*, since he is the one critic of the novel Greene says he ever learned anything from.[18]

Lubbock seeks to determine how a novel is made. At least implicitly, he raises three questions. What is the novelist's intention? Does he fulfill it? If so, is it worthwhile? The first question we have already answered. The third need only be considered if the answer to the preceding one is in the affirmative. And so to the second. I feel Greene fails to make the most of his subject, because he fails to see Scobie whole. Greene is merely acquainted with Scobie, whereas he is intimate with the Priest. The Priest has a real dilemma thrust upon him, as Richard Vorhees observes: "He does not, like Scobie, create a false dilemma to satisfy his masochism."[19]

How does Greene himself see Scobie? He sees Scobie as a just man whose sins seem to flow inevitably from an unselfish sense of pity. Here is the real paradox of the epigraph as Greene presents it: justice and selflessness related to sin as cause and effect. Greene's intention with respect to Scobie was to show how a good man may be betrayed and trapped by his very virtues. But this intention is not borne out; Greene fails

[18] Paul Rostenne, *Graham Greene: témoin des temps tragiques*, p. 11. In a letter-preface, Greene cites the enormous influence exercised in England on his generation by *The Craft of Fiction*.

[19] Vorhees, *op. cit.*, p. 398.

to see that Scobie's cancerous pity kills his sense of justice and his unselfishness before he commits adultery, murder, sacrilege, and suicide. *Prior* to his commission of these mortal sins, his virtue is dead.

As we saw in connection with *The Ministry of Fear*, Greene is harsh on pity, because "pity is a terrible thing. . . . Pity is the worst passion of all: we don't outlive it like sex." Admittedly, Greene's denunciation of Rowe's pity in *The Ministry of Fear* is more emphatic than his denunciation of Scobie's, as this passage—Greene's strongest condemnation of Scobie's pity—shows: "Pity smouldered like decay at his [Scobie's] heart. He would never rid himself of it." In both works, nonetheless, Greene exposes the folly of pity. To assume in practice that Greene ever regards pity—however theoretically confused he may be about it in *The Heart of the Matter*—as anything more than a corruption of love is to misread him.[20]

Scobie's human relationships are all based on pity. He "couldn't shut his eyes or his ears to any human need of him." His sense of responsibility moves away from "the beautiful and the graceful and the intelligent. They could find their own way. It was the face for which nobody would go out of his way, the face that would never catch the covert look, the face which would soon be used to rebuffs and indifference that demanded his allegiance." His discontented wife and his pathetic mistress are the chief victims demanding allegiance. After swearing to preserve his wife Louise's happiness, he does so with indifferent success until he accepts another and contra-

[20] Donat O'Donnell's failure, in *Maria Cross* (New York, Oxford, 1952), to note Greene's actual condemnation of Scobie's pity, and O'Donnell's consequent assumption that Greene identifies pity with charity or love leads him to charge Greene with being wasteful of his subject (p. 86). As the reader has seen, I agree that Greene fails to carry out his intention but for a different reason.

dictory responsibility, his mistress Helen's happiness. Scobie begins by pitying one woman and ends by pitying God. In the middle of the journey, this "terrible impotent feeling of responsibility and pity" so gnaws at him that he wonders "if one knew . . . the facts, would one have to feel pity even for the planets? if one reached what they called the heart of the matter?"

It is significant that women almost exclusively comprise the group that Scobie's pity exploits. Injustice when it is meted out to a woman—Louise or Helen chiefly—invariably draws his pitying attitude as a poultice draws a boil. He does not hesitate to compare the suffering of Louise and Helen with that of Christ. But he is curiously unmoved, or moved to a far less degree, by male disaster. And it is not that there is a shortage of unsuccessful, unattractive men waiting to be deformed by Scobie's pity. The contrary is true: Scobie comes into contact with far more rejected men than women. Why does he not take on Harris or Wilson, for instance, both of whom are lonely exiles, immature, unhappy, suffering from feelings of inferiority—or any of a dozen other eligible males? The truth is that Scobie is abnormally sensitive to the whims of women, has too much respect for them, and is emotionally subservient to them. At times, he even identifies himself with them. "He felt oddly unmanned, lying in bed alone waiting for Louise to join him." Without lust, he commits adultery. His lugubrious affair with Helen is undertaken by Scobie not to allay concupiscence but to save her from what he considers a worse fate—the philandering Bagster, and despair. He is the self-appointed guardian of the happiness of certain women, and he uses sexual intimacy to reassure them.

Lest the sympathy extended by Scobie to the Portuguese sea captain caught smuggling a letter be cited as an exception, let it be remembered that Scobie shows no mercy until the captain alludes to his daughter. Later, Scobie admits to himself "that had been the turning point, the daughter," the unattractive daughter. Indeed, any time Scobie pities a man it is for the sake of a woman or for the sake of a child. His secondary emotional identification is with children and childhood. Perhaps that is why life seems immeasurably long to him. "Couldn't the test of man have been carried out in fewer years? Couldn't we have committed our first major sin at seven, have ruined ourselves for love or hate at ten, have clutched at redemption on a fifteen-year-old death bed?" Looking at the corpse of Pemberton, a young man who has hanged himself, Scobie "had the impression that he was looking at a child in a night-shirt quietly asleep: the pimples were the pimples of puberty and the dead face seemed to bear the trace of no experience beyond the class-room or the football field. 'Poor child,' he said aloud."[21]

Neurotic Scobie mixes religion with pity to make the combination sound noble to himself. He misuses religion to rationalize his position that his sins help others. The Church's exhortation to the faithful to see the lineaments of Christ in any suffering human being is distorted by Scobie to mean that he personally must assume entire responsibility for all suffering. The exhortation to regard a vow as sacred prompts Scobie,

[21] Donat O'Donnell, in a profound if somewhat unconvincing essay on *The Heart of the Matter,* reaches a similar conclusion, even though his premises are radically different from mine. "Scobie is a crucified man: he sees himself . . . as Christ on the cross. And the cross for him is female and sentient—Louise—Helen—and we have the equilibrium of pain inflicted and endured, the longing for death. . . . What Scobie pities—what he is nailed to—is his own childhood: that is the cross into which his wife and his mistress have to turn." (*Maria Cross*, pp. 252-253.)

who does not do things by half, to take a casual promise of assistance to Helen as seriously as he does his marital vow. The Church's mandate to perform charitable deeds is construed by Scobie as sufficient reason not to put his own soul first and not to trust in God's mercy to the one—Louise or Helen—he might abandon. The mandate to love thy neighbor as thyself is interpreted by Scobie to mean that he must offer his own damnation as a loving sacrifice for others—Louise, Helen, the dying six-year-old survivor of a shipwreck, even God. The ways in which Scobie misuses religion to rationalize his problem could be multiplied, but the conclusion is perfectly clear already. Scobie is a hilt man: he falsifies religion by pushing moral precepts to an illogical extreme.

Maurice Bendrix, the novelist in *The End of the Affair*, reflecting on his art, commends the character who takes charge. Scobie is that kind of character—only Scobie goes too far. Greene, as we have seen, intended Scobie to illustrate a paradox about sin and Christianity. But as the story develops it takes a turn that appears to contradict, or at least to disregard, the author's original design. As Greene told himself the story of Scobie, as he became more acquainted with the subject of *The Heart of the Matter*, he apparently discovered more in it than he could cope with. Specifically, Greene does not seem to have sufficiently perceived that Scobie is a very sick man.[22] I contend that *The Heart of the Matter* would be a truer, finer, more vivid, and more forceful picture of life if Greene had made more of Scobie's neurotic attitude toward suffering and his neurotic sympathy for the plight of women and children and less use of jumbled theology. The theological problem presented by the novel does not find satisfactory expression in

[22] According to Marcel Moré, Scobie is a neurasthenic. "The Two Holocausts of Scobie," *Cross Currents*, II (1951), 48.

the drama of Scobie. To the extent that the novel is a failure, however, the failure is largely literary: Greene fails to explore fully the potential meanings in the body of experience presented in *The Heart of the Matter*. The psychological ambiguity *in* the Priest secures the optimum effect for his story; an ambiguity in the facts presented about Scobie does not obtain what one critic calls "the enriching ambiguity in which possible meanings are superimposed and intermingle, but an ambiguity of irresolution."[23]

Sarah Miles, in *The End of the Affair*, is as altruistic as Major Scobie. She loves to help people and wants to suffer in the place of others. She wants to offer up inordinate sacrifices for those she loves: her husband, Henry, her lover, Maurice, her admirer, Smythe. To be of use to them is her sole desire. Sarah beseeches God: "Teach me to love. I don't mind my pain. It's their pain I can't stand. Let my pain go on and on, but stop theirs. Dear God, if only You could come down from Your cross for a while and let me get up there instead. If I could suffer like You, I could heal like You." Despite these similarities, Sarah is no female Scobie: she learns what he never learns —trust. Scobie trusts no one, not even God. Sarah trusts God most of all. Because she gradually surrenders self-will, Sarah is heaven-bound; because he stubbornly plays the role of a pseudo-providence to the end, Scobie is not. In other words, Sarah's charity is not dissipated by self-pity masquerading as compassion.

The more Sarah falls in love with God, the more Maurice Bendrix, her rejected lover, falls in hate. Father Crompton tells Bendrix that he is a good hater. Bendrix admits it. "I'm in hate. I hate Sarah because she was a whore, I hate Henry because

[23] O'Donnell, *op. cit.*, p. 81.

she stuck to him, and I hate you [Father Crompton] and your imaginary God because you took her away from all of us." On the wings of violence, God first intervenes in the affair. The struggle between religious fervor and carnal love commences in the heart of Sarah on a night of the London blitz when a bomb hit buries Maurice beneath the debris. Believing him dead, she prays for his resurrection, adding a vow to give him up if only he be allowed to live. When her lover crawls out, only superficially injured, the amazed women is convinced her prayer has been answered. Then comes the agony over whether she is bound to a promise to a God in Whom she had only wavering belief. As the adulterous affection is gradually transmuted into a consuming love of the Almighty, she concludes that she is.

The epigraph for *The End of the Affair* is taken from Léon Bloy: "Man has places in his heart which do not yet exist, and into them enters suffering in order that they may have existence." Greene here intends to show that goodness can be achieved in this world, but only through suffering. His success is partial. In the matter of technique, *The End of the Affair* is impressive; less so in the matter of character presentation: Sarah's diary—trite device that this could be—is not a forced contrivance, but her sanctity is largely rhetorical. Since the former judgment requires far less examination than the latter, let me consider the diary first. To begin with, the use of a diary is a device often employed by Greene's French Catholic contemporaries. Witness Bernanos' use of it in *Journal d'un curé de campagne* and Mauriac's in *Le Noeud de vipères*. Mauriac indeed goes well beyond Greene. He asks the reader to accept the unlikely coincidence that the two leading characters would each keep a diary. In view of this, Sarah's diary does not seem contrived; besides, I am not sure that Sarah's dilemma could have been convincingly projected any other way. And this leads me back to my objection.

While complaining that Sarah's sanctity is explained for the most part rather than exhibited, I must not leave out of consideration the nature of Sarah's bargain with God. The vow she takes necessitates giving up Maurice. This automatically eliminates *external* conflict, the sensual struggle of man and woman, from the novel and substitutes *internal* conflict, the spiritual struggle of the soul with God. Sensual encounters are readily dramatizable; spiritual encounters less so. To persuade his readers—so as to make them feel it—of a major change for the better in a character is one of the hardest things for any novelist to do. Even so great a novel as *Crime and Punishment* is a case in point. Raskolnikov's reformation, following the realization of his guilt through the sin of pride, is the least convincing part of the novel. The fact that the author devotes so little space to Raskolnikov's actual expiation can be taken as a sign that even Dostoyevsky was unsure of his ability to bring this kind of metamorphosis off convincingly. Admittedly he is more successful, perhaps completely successful, with Alyosha in *The Brothers Karamazov*. But here Dostoyevsky is not starting with a great sinner—the uphill pull is a lot shorter. Even the major change for the better that takes place in Sonia, in *Crime and Punishment*, is largely explained, not exhibited. The analogy with Dostoyevsky is not intended to excuse Greene but to highlight the difficulties involved in portraying the spiritual growth of a character.

The difference between "showing" an incident in fiction and merely reporting it is subjective and relative, anyway. By comparison with Sigrid Undset's Kristin Lavransdatter, for example, Sarah seems a hazy character; but by comparison with T. S. Eliot's Celia, she seems not at all faraway and unreal. We do not eavesdrop on Celia's surge to sanctity in *The Cocktail Party*. We are simply told she becomes a saint, and we are left to guess at her motivation. Her conversion has to be taken entirely on faith. At least Greene makes Sarah's motivation clear, and we do get to witness the incident that triggers her conversion. Even to the death, which he merely reports, Eliot's character drawing of Celia remains wholly discursive. And since suffering martyrdom by crucifixion, as Celia does, is a more spectacular manner of death than just taking a fever and dying in bed, as Sarah does, Eliot has far less excuse than Greene for not "showing" it.

If we can generalize from the examples of Dostoyevsky and Eliot, it would seem that even greater writers than Greene fly unevenly in their effort to range the heavens from the lowest altitude to the highest. The longer the ascent, the higher the altitude, the less graceful is the flight. Greene is no different: the more his story soars upward the more it lurches. To have expected Greene to succeed in the last fifty pages is to have expected him to succeed where some greater writers fail. As soon as Greene introduces God as a character and solves human problems by miracles he dooms his achievement as pure literature, for the machinery from which the rescuing God emerges is less the novelist's than the theologian's. The reader smells smoke as long as the fire of passion rages, but as soon as Greene puts it out and lights the paschal candle the smell abates. The vow, since it douses Sarah's passion and prepares her for her contemplation of the Passion—which is well-nigh undramatizable on the terms Greene sets for himself—is an unfortunate literary device.

I am not finding fault with the means Greene chooses to purify Sarah. It is perfectly valid to have Sarah purified by devotion to God. But it is too bad Greene could not manage it in less discursive terms. When regeneration is accomplished by less overt reliance on the supernatural, the result is usually more satisfactory. Consider the regeneration of Anna Christie, for instance. This slatternly barge captain's daughter is rescued from her shameful past by the devotion of a brawling, fluent Irish sailor and by the calm majesty of the sea. Even here God is undoubtedly the Purifier, but O'Neill sees God working through intermediaries—man and nature. This is not to say that God's ways are always devious, that He never intervenes directly in the affairs of mankind: it is only to say that when the artist chooses to depict God's direct intervention he does so at his own risk.

III

In a short story included in his second collection of short stories, *A Sense of Reality* (1963), Greene has one of the characters maintain that true literary criticism leaves the author's views out of account. "A novel is made up of words and characters. Are the words well chosen and do the characters live? All the rest belongs to literary gossip."[24] But a critic cannot act on this advice; it leaves out of consideration the fact that the words an author chooses and the characters he creates depend upon his views. A critic must pay attention to problems of theme.

Greene never states his themes. He simply illustrates them in terms of the characters and the action. Since he lives passionately in his ideas, his literary works never suffer from being abstract. It would embarrass him, he confesses, to discuss the ideas underlying his novels; because, in the act of writing, he is carried along by the unpredictable energies of his characters, rather than by the desire to express his thoughts

[24] "A Visit to Morin," p. 67.

about the problems besetting mankind.[25] Grace, sin, and the flesh, Greene's central preoccupations, are presented paradoxically. Those characters who are the recipients of grace—for not all of Greene's characters are—sin more than the non-recipients. The way into the supernatural starts from the depths of sin. The body is corrupt, but it also has religious significance.

Every novelist tries to treat significant human experience, but the Catholic novelist tries to treat it at its roots—where God confronts man and grace encounters free will. Grace can act like a thunderbolt or grace can act like a leaven. Some of Greene's characters are struck by grace on the road to Damascus. Like Paul's—"as once at a crash"—Sarah's conversion is quick and dramatic. Others of Greene's characters are gradually transformed by grace on the road to Carthage. Like Austin's—"a lingering-out sweet skill"[26]—the Priest's rehabilitation is slow and secret.

Among modern Catholic novelists only Mauriac conveys the triumph of grace with artistic skill comparable to Greene's. All Mauriac's action, like Greene's, is wound around the spool of sin and despair, salvaged only by a wretched, but indomitable, faith in the liberating grace of God. The comparison has been made most effectively by a critic: "More violently and perhaps more mysteriously than Mauriac, he [Greene] has joined his work with Catholicism. The debate he carries on is the oldest in the world—that between nature and grace. It is the debate of man placed between two worlds: an inaccessible heaven and earth heavy and rich with the life it bears."[27]

[25] Rostenne, *op. cit.*, pp. 11-12.
[26] Gerard Manley Hopkins, "The Wreck of the Deutschland," stanza 10.
[27] Wallace Fowlie, Review of *The Lost Childhood*, in the *New York Times*, February 17, 1952, Sec. 7, p. 31.

The agonies of sin—usually sins of the flesh—may shatter the sinner's complacency and reveal to him for the first time his lack of self-sufficiency and his need for God. In this way, carnal passion may be transformed finally into religious passion. So it is with Greene's Sarah Miles and Mauriac's Gisele de Plailly: these two erring women, responding to grace, turn from debauchery to the Infinite.

In implying that some characters are offered grace by God while others are not, Greene, however, parts company with Mauriac, who has no such neo-Calvinistic division. Greene is generous in making grace available in abundance to all the Catholic characters, even demoniacal Pinkie, but he is stingy where certain non-Catholic characters are concerned. Though it is denied them for different reasons, Ida and the police lieutenant are the two outstanding examples of characters to whom grace is denied. The Lieutenant is cut off from grace, because, warring with God, he hates Christianity; Ida is cut off, because, indifferent to God, she ignores Christianity. Conflict in Greene's two-world view is generated by the antagonism which always exists between these characters who are given no access to God's grace and those who are. But this central contrast, more pronounced in *Brighton Rock* than in *The Power and the Glory,* has heretical implications: for the orthodox Catholic all virtues spring from grace. Ida's justice and the Lieutenant's compassion are no exception. To believe, as Greene obviously does, that some characters are forever outside the pale of grace, and so incapable of religious belief and experience, is to cast a gratuitous slur on God's mercy and to flirt with Jansenism. Greene's position here is inconsistent, because ordinarily he follows Pascal in setting no limits to God's mercy.

The Tertullian contrast in Greene's fiction "between the

supernatural man who lives on the plane of good and evil and the natural man who lives on the plane of right and wrong" has been put concisely by Francis X. Connolly. He justifiably complains that "right and wrong are not really opposed to good and evil; the same God who created the supernatural order created the natural order. Grace perfects nature. Natural goodness invites the free gift of grace. Greene's whole emphasis, however, would tend to suggest that it is bad to be right, bad to be cheerful, healthy, companionable. There is a trace of savage Manicheism in his resentment of well-being."[28] Now the unorthodoxy in Greene's novels would not be important from a literary point of view, provided his world seemed entirely authentic. But that is not the case in *Brighton Rock* or (though to a lesser extent) in *The Power and the Glory*. The imaginative cohesion of these two books is disrupted by the assumption that not everyone receives grace. Helen Gardner rightly contends that Pinkie, Rose, and the Priest are falsely romanticized and Ida and the Lieutenant falsely turned into semi-caricatures on account of it.[29]

Greene does not swallow Jansenism whole, however. If he did, Ida and the Lieutenant would be his greatest sinners; for according to Jansen those who are not offered grace cannot help sinning. Yet the only commandments Ida breaks, the first and the sixth, are the only commandments Pinkie keeps. And the Lieutenant, starved for grace, is a Lilliputian sinner by comparison with the Priest. It is the pessimism of Jansenism that is most endemic in Greene.

Not only are the Catholic characters greater sinners, but they are frequently less happy in the state of grace than they

[28] Connolly, *op. cit.*, p. 20.
[29] "François Mauriac: A Woman of the Pharisees," *Penguin New Writing*, XXXI (1947), 102.

are in the state of sin. Sarah Miles, for instance, is a carefree, relaxed sinner before her conversion and life of virtue plunge her into woe. The nearer she approaches to God the less joy she takes from the created world and human love. Pascal in his *Pensées* describes the wretchedness of man without God; Greene describes the wretchedness of man with God.

It is interesting to compare Greene in this with Evelyn Waugh. In *Brideshead Revisited* the virtuous Catholics, with the exception of Cordelia, are a miserable lot. To be in love with God made Chaucer's Parson happy; it only makes Cordelia's brother, Brideshead, and her mother, Lady Marchmain, melancholy. Waugh, like Greene, shuts his ears to Yeats' line "For the good are always the merry."[30] Indeed the reverse is depicted: for Cara, the mistress of Lord Marchmain, takes the most joy out of life. And the most contented of all Greene's characters is jolly Ida, the woman of easy virtue.

Happiness, Greene implies, is incompatible with grace. No good can come of happiness. "Happiness," he advises in *The Ministry of Fear*, "should always be qualified by a knowledge of misery." Success too is suspect; a sense of doom hovers over it. "One looked around and saw the doomed everywhere— the champion runner who one day would sag over the tape; the head of the school who would atone, poor devil, during forty dreary undistinguished years; the scholar . . . and when success began to touch oneself too, however mildly, one could only pray that failure would not be held off for too long."[31] Close to the heart of Greene's upside-down matter is Sean O'Faolain's witty observation concerning him: "Joyfully he reverses Browning. God's in his heaven, all's wrong

---

[30] *Collected Poems* (New York, Macmillan, 1947), p. 84.
[31] *The Lost Childhood*, p. 16.

with the world."[32] Greene reminds us of a reformed card player who is reputed to have given up poker because he drew too many inside straights.

"Goodness has only once found a perfect incarnation in a human body and never will again, but evil can always find a home there," Greene writes in *The Lost Childhood*. The ease with which "evil can always find a home" in the human body is due to original sin. Greene reflects his considered commitment to the doctrine of original sin by quoting these words —some of which have been alluded to earlier—from Cardinal Newman's *Apologia pro vita sua* in the epigraph to *Another Mexico:*

. . . The defeat of good, the success of evil, physical pain, mental anguish, the prevalence and intensity of sin, the pervading idolatries, the corruptions, the dreary hopeless irreligion . . . —all this is a vision to dizzy and appall; and inflicts upon the mind the sense of a profound mystery, which is absolutely beyond human solution.

What shall be said to this heart-piercing, reason-bewildering fact? I can only answer, that either there is no Creator, or this living society of men is in a true sense discarded from His presence . . . *if* there be a God, *since* there is a God, the human race is implicated in some terrible aboriginal calamity.

For all this, Greene does not exaggerate the results of original sin. He never portrays man as so mired in sin as to be beyond the power of redemption. Those of his characters who are most strongly committed to sin always retain their freedom to renounce it, to respond to the tug of divine grace. Grace tries to get at the dying Scobie in the passage, "all the

[32] *The Vanishing Hero* (Boston, Little, Brown, 1957), p. 47.

time outside the house . . . someone wandered, seeking to get in. . . ." Even Pinkie, who has on his face the flush of the flames, recognizes before the end a counterpull, an enormous emotion beating on him. "It was like something trying to get in, the presence of gigantic wings against the glass." The reader hears the fluttering of the wings of grace, the feathered glory striving to caress him, as the Boy disappears.

All of Greene's Catholic characters regard sin as an outrage perpetrated against the person of Christ. Contemplating his sins, Scobie "had a sudden picture before his eyes of a bleeding face, of eyes closed by the continuous shower of blows: the punch-drunk head of God reeling sideways." This frighteningly anthropomorphic description finds a restrained counterpart in a passage from Waugh's *Brideshead Revisited*. In a self-flagellating speech, Julia Flyte, a bad Catholic, shows her agnostic lover what their sin means:

Christ dying with it, nailed hand and foot; hanging over the bed in the night nursery; hanging year after year in the dark little study at Farm Street with the shining oilcloth; hanging in the dark church where only the old charwoman raises the dust and one candle burns; hanging at noon among the crowds and the soldiers; no comfort but a sponge of vinegar and the kind words of a thief; hanging forever; never the cool sepulcher and the grave clothes spread on the stone slab, never the oil and spices in the dark cave; always the midday sun and the dice clicking for the seamless coat.[33]

There is plenty of opportunity for Greene's characters to familiarize themselves with the significance of sin: it is intoxicatingly omnipresent. Even in infancy they exhale the scent of sin and corruption. Vaughan, Wordsworth, and De La Mare felt that each human creature is most truly in

[33] *Brideshead Revisited* (Boston, Little, Brown, 1946), p. 288.

harmony with the universe in childhood. They described childhood as a wonderfully direct apprehension of the truth, only gradually dulled by doubt and poisoned by experience. With its emphasis on the *gradual* loss of innocence, this description of childhood would not find favor with Greene's characters. Pinkie, for one, refuses to equate innocence with childhood. "You had to go back a long way further before you got innocence; innocence was a slobbering mouth, a toothless gum pulling at the teats, perhaps not even that; innocence was the ugly cry of birth." Pinkie reverses Wordsworth. "He trailed the clouds of his own glory after him: hell lay about him in his infancy."

The prison shades of grown-up disillusionment were also expedited by and for Greene himself. Teeming with sin and corruption, his own childhood was just as smoky as Pinkie's, if less pathetic, and was marred by some of the same kind of irrational violence. The shocking story, drawn from his own experience, that Greene tells in *Another Mexico* of the suicide of a fifteen-year-old girl, pregnant out-of-wedlock, anticipates a similar version recited by Pinkie. Adumbrating the "faint secret sensual pleasure" which Pinkie feels, fingering a bottle of vitriol, as Rose approaches, is the sadistic impulse experienced by Greene at the age of fourteen, as reflected in a passage from *Journey without Maps:* "There was a girl lodging close by I wanted to do things to; I loitered outside the door hoping to see her. I didn't do anything about it, I wasn't old enough, but I was happy; I could think about pain as something desirable and not as something dreaded. It was as if I had discovered that the way to enjoy life was to appreciate pain."

In their degrees, all Greene's Catholic heroes and heroines are sinners; even those of them who eventually reach blessedness have en route been perilously close to damning themselves. Pinkie, one of the most Satanic characters in modern fiction, provides us with a clue as to why Greene has never created a figure of absolute goodness. Pinkie, Greene's first memorable image of the character he had so cherished as a boy in *The Viper of Milan*—"perfect evil walking the world where perfect good can never walk again"[34]—is black in a universe where the best human specimens are not white, but grey. Greene's practice at this point—concentrating exclusively on the love of God as it shines forth among the sinful—is in marked contrast to the practice of Georges Bernanos, who has no such compunction about portraying both extremes of the human spectrum. He populates his world with demons—M. Guérou in *L'Imposture*, the Abbé Cénabre in *La Joie*, and M. Ouine—and saints—the diarist of *Journal d'un curé de campagne*, the Abbé Donissan in *Sous le soleil de Satan*, Chantal de la Clergerie in *La Joie*, and the Abbé Chevance in *L'Imposture*. Thus Bernanos remembers what Greene forgets: that God is also loved by the sinless.

In limiting his universe to sinners, François Mauriac, who here resembles Greene rather than his countryman Bernanos, defends the practice on the grounds that sinless Catholics, virgins and saints—such as the Little Flower and the Curé d'Ars—are not fit material for the art of the novel. "But how is one to describe the secret drama of a man who struggles to subdue his earthly heritage, that drama which finds expression neither in words nor gestures? Where is the artist who may dare to imagine the processes and shifts of that great protagonist—Grace? It is the mark of our slavery and of our wretchedness that we can, without lying, paint a faithful portrait only of the passions."[35] Certainly Greene acts on this assumption.

---

[34] *The Lost Childhood*, p. 17.
[35] *The Enemy* (New York, Holt, 1949), p. 279.

Never attempting a portrait of unsullied goodness, he works solely with imperfect human material. Like Mauriac, he is the novelist of the weak, the suffering, the misunderstood. His pity for all the exiled of the world and his rooted interest in the seedy makes him temperamentally ill-adapted to be the novelist of a sinless world.

It is not the intention of this essay to criticize the critics of Greene, and yet for a few pages it will be necessary to do just that in order to correct what seems to me a crucial misunderstanding of Greene's position on sin and sinners. Most commentators persist in attributing to Greene a view on the relationship of sin to virtue that I find little basis for. And nearly all of them, in my judgment, err in their interpretation of Greene's attitude towards various kinds of sinners.

In the short story "A Visit to Morin," Morin, a Catholic novelist whom Greene obviously intends to be identified with himself, is plagued by critics who applied the word "paradox" to his work "with an air of disapproval" and "seemed to scent heresy like a rat dead somewhere under the boards. . . ." In an effort to locate the exact spot, critics have pulled up nearly all of Greene's floor boards. On occasion I have wielded a crowbar, too; but when Kenneth Tynan imputes to Greene the paradoxical idea "that sin holds within it the seeds of virtue,"[36] I think it is time to put a halt to housewrecking.

This glorification of sin and the accompanying notion that the sinner somehow occupies a privileged place in the world have been termed "sin mysticism."[37] Herbert Haber docu-

[36] "An Inner View of Graham Greene," *Harper's Bazaar*, February 1953, p. 128.

[37] "Sin mysticism" is a trend associated with what, in Catholic circles, was formerly called "la nouvelle théologie." In an allocution to the Fédération Mondiale des Jeunesses Féminines Catholiques, His Holiness, the late Pope Pius XII, condemned it.

ments Greene's purported "sin mysticism" at length. Analyzing the character of the Priest, Haber concludes that the Priest "found the path 'to the good death,' to martyrdom and saint-hood, through an immersion into the pentecostal flame of earthly sin. . . . Through adultery, the Priest finds in himself the capacity for love: he does indeed love the twisted fruit of that transgression—his child, Brigida. Through drunkenness, he becomes humble to the point of ungratuitous self-effacement."[38]

This type of criticism assumes that the Priest's humility and selfless love have been caused by alcoholism and fornication. But it is faulty to perceive a cause and effect relationship where a mere priority in time exists. The Priest and, for that matter, Sarah, also, grow spiritually not because they have sinned—sin is not the condition for their virtue—but because they have been engulfed by disaster, purified by pain. The Priest's complacency is corroded by persecution; Sarah's lust by the self-enforced loss of Maurice. In other words, Greene is exalting the whisky priest, not his whisky-guzzling. Nor is it the sensuality and unfaithfulness of Sarah that Greene extols; it is her self-control in the face of enormous temptation. It was after all the penitence of Magdalen, not her promiscuity, which won her salvation.

The sinner, never the sin, enlists Greene's sympathies. And even then it is only a special kind of sinner that Greene takes an interest in: the sinner, in Péguy's paradox (previously alluded to), who, together with the saint, is at the heart of Christendom.[39] Guilt-riven and tormented, this sinner is a

[38] "The Two Worlds of Graham Greene," *Modern Fiction Studies*, III (Autumn 1957), 266.

[39] Jacques Maritain echoes a variation of this: ". . . in practice there are only two ways to know the depths of things: the way of sinners and the way of saints." *This is My Philosophy*, ed. Whit Burnett (New York, Harper, 1957), p. 251.

recurrent figure in the art of many modern Catholic writers —Bloy, Claudel, Mauriac—who invariably endow him with two characteristics. He never abandons himself to sin without a soul-tearing struggle, and he continually fights his bondage. Far better than the externally pious Christian, who is smug about his success in keeping the commandments, the guilt-riven, tormented sinner knows that Christ alone can save him. Neither Greene nor the others are celebrating "sin as an incitement to salvation"[40] but rather the weakness of man and the power of God. Greene does not glorify sin; he glorifies humility. The Priest's love for Christ, like that of Peter the prototype of all priests, is not augmented by his betrayal but by the sorrow that ensues from the betrayal.

Greene follows St. Thomas Aquinas in considering sins of pride worse than sins of the flesh.[41] If Greene seems too lenient towards fornication and adultery, it is solely as a reaction to the apotheosis of invincible complacency.

Alexander Boyle's judgment on Greene's art illustrates the general misunderstanding on this point. "There is a sort of inverted Phariseeism . . . which not only welcomes to its bosom the thief, the prostitute, and the murderer, but assigns as their portion indifference and contempt to those whose feet have rarely wandered from the path traced out before them at their First Communion."[42] Granted that Greene welcomes thieves, prostitutes, and murderers—in keeping with the Christian attitude of hating the sin but loving the sinner— and vouchsafes them a future; he does not assign contempt to the sinless for the obvious reason that his universe is limited

---

[40] Kenneth Tynan, "An Inner View of Graham Greene," *Harper's Bazaar*, February 1953, p. 128.

[41] *Summa Theologica* II-II, q. 162, a. 7.

[42] "The Symbolism of Graham Greene," *Irish Monthly*, March 1952, p. 102.

to sinners. Although Boyle cites no examples to bolster his contention, Elizabeth Sewell, in a similar indictment, uses as evidence the pious woman in the Mexican prison (*The Power and the Glory*) and Aunt Helen (*The Living Room*).[43] Admittedly Greene has no sympathy whatever for either of them, but he does not flail them for the reasons Miss Sewell supposes—bourgeois virtue, spiritual mediocrity. On the contrary, he denies them virtue, even mediocrity: he denigrates them for their self-righteousness, their cancerous pride "that puffeth up," and their outward piety, which hypocritically masks an unholy meanness of spirit.

To identify Greene as an exponent of "sin mysticism," as Dietrich von Hildebrand does,[44] and to assume that Greene's Catholic novels imply that humility presupposes sin and that alcoholism or adultery are indispensable protections against pharisaism is to misread them. This assumption overlooks the fact that the privations of persecution, quite apart from his sensational sins, are enough to humble the Priest. Furthermore, on the morning of his execution the Priest begs God's pardon for *all* his sins and realizes "now . . . at the end there was only one thing that counted—to be a saint." Where Scobie is concerned this assumption ignores the fact that he is more humble, in the sense of experiencing less moral superiority, *before* his adulterous liaison. Greene does not sprinkle holy water on sin or endow it with the character of a *felix culpa* or invite someone to sin with the hope of bringing about good results. Instead he instills a reverence for the individual person despite his sin and cultivates a more profound respect for

---

[43] "The Imagination of Graham Greene," *Thought*, XXIX (Spring 1954), 56.

[44] *True Morality and Its Counterfeits* (New York, McKay, 1955), pp. 3, 11.

the mysterious transforming powers of grace which can enable a penitent thief on the cross to "steal" paradise.

Human love is impotent: Rose cannot save Pinkie from destroying himself; the Priest cannot save his natural daughter from corruption; Louise and Helen cannot save Scobie from suicide, and he cannot save them from unhappiness. Divine love is potent: the martyrdom of the Priest miraculously saves the boy Luis—and by implication all the children of Tabasco —from communism; the sanctity of Sarah miraculously saves Parkis' boy from death and Smythe from further humiliation. Human love, in Greene's eyes, is often at odds with divine love. "This is what human love had done to him [Scobie]— it had robbed him of love for eternity."

Physical love is Ida's promiscuity, Rose's indiscretion with Pinkie, the Priest's despairful act with Maria, Scobie's duty toward his wife and mistress, and Sarah's affair. Passion is vulgar, naive, guilt-ridden, tedious, lugubrious, or compulsive but never very attractive. Save in the case of Rose, the sexual act is not motivated by love; save in the case of Sarah, the sexual act is not even motivated by lust. Called in to counterbalance the deficiencies of passion, the love of God is a blessing for some of these characters, a deception for others. Ultimately the Priest and Sarah seek supernatural love for its own sake and in so doing naturally perfect their human love also. On the other hand, Scobie uses supernatural love as an excuse to avoid committing himself to human love. This evasion is the kind of "love," as expressed in *The Ministry of Fear*, that "helps to make imperceptible the imprisonment of a man." Rose pits God-love against man-love and decides for the latter. On the probability that Pinkie has not made heaven, she wants never to go there. To the old priest in confession, she insists: "I want to be like him—damned."

The Catholic character who does not perfect himself in charity associates the flesh with revulsion. Ida's big breasts pointing through a thin summer dress stir Pinkie's disgust. Louise sitting up in bed under a mosquito net reminds Scobie "of a joint under a meat cover." And Helen in a comparable position reminds him of "a bundle of cannon fodder." On the other hand, the character who perfects himself in charity, far from detesting the flesh, sees the body as sanctified. The implications of the Incarnation—finding Christ in his fellow men and, particularly and painfully, in those in whom His image was grotesquely distorted by sin and shame—exhilarate the Priest. "At the centre of his own faith there always stood the convincing mystery—that we were made in God's image— God was the parent, but He was also the policeman, the criminal, the priest, the maniac and the judge. Something resembling God dangled from the gibbet or went into odd attitudes before the bullets in a prison yard or contorted itself like a camel in the attitude of sex." Sarah too pushes beyond the truth that the essence of man's likeness to God is intellectual and spiritual and wonders: "Could anybody love Him or hate Him if He hadn't got a body?" Revering the body, despite its capacity for sin, she poses the question: "We can love with our minds, but can we love only with our minds? Love extends itself all the time, so that we can even love with our senseless nails; we love even with our clothes, so that a sleeve can feel a sleeve."

As far as Greene's own attitude toward the flesh is concerned, many critics imply that he ought to pray with Baudelaire: "Lord, give me the strength and courage to contemplate my heart and my body without disgust."[45] Elizabeth Sewell turns her indictment on a paradox. "The body is seen as corrupted, yet sensuality is sadly pursued and given almost a religious significance."[46] William Birmingham's summation—"Greene's puritanism lies in his choice of metaphor in the expression not only of sexual relationships but all bodily activities as well"[47]—foreshadows the Tynan whim that Greene turns out the lights whenever he undresses.[48] In describing the love-making of his characters it is true that Greene often employs images of death, but usually these images are compatible with the character: so that when Scobie, lying alongside Helen, has an illusion about her—"She lay in the odd cramped attitude of someone who has been shot in escaping"—this illusion is congruous with his own death-wish. In any case, in a note that I received from Greene in 1957, he flatly states, "I would never regard the body as revolting." And in an essay on the headmaster of Rugby, written much earlier, he complains that "it would be possible to read Mr. Lyon without ever guessing that sexual intercourse was pleasant or amusing."[49] Later in the same essay, Greene argues that every student should be taught "that sexual enjoyment is neither solemn nor dull."

These declarations are certainly not in keeping with Greene's alleged puritanism. How little puritanical he really is, is evident as soon as he is contrasted with Mauriac. The latter is committed to the myth that the flesh is wholly evil,

[45] "Journey to Cythera," *The Flowers of Evil* (New York, New Directions, 1955), p. 163.
[46] "The Imagination of Graham Greene," *Thought*, XXIX (Spring 1954), 55.
[47] William Birmingham, *op. cit.*, pp. 87-88.
[48] Tynan, *op. cit.*, p. 128.
[49] *The Old School* (London, Jonathon Cape, 1934), p. 250.

and all carnal love, even in marriage, is guilty. He quotes with approval Pascal's definition of marriage as "The lowest of the conditions of Christianity, vile and prejudicial in the eyes of God," and he speaks, in his life of Racine, of "that certitude fatal to human happiness, that carnal love is evil, evil which we cannot help committing."[50] It would be fatuous, of course, to contend that we are dealing with polar extremes here—say Calvin and D. H. Lawrence; in truth the difference between Mauriac and Greene is a difference in degree: so that Greene's characters, failing to equate love-making with ecstasy, are as often depressed by it as exhilarated. Yet, and this is the important point, they do expect relatively more from sexual love than Mauriac's characters ever do. This is most clearly seen by juxtaposing the view of Mauriac's Brigitte—"All the miseries of our human state come from our inability to remain chaste"[51]—with the view of Greene's D.—"It was something to be in love with a living woman, even if you get nothing from it but fear, jealousy, pain. It was not an ignoble emotion."

IV

Although Graham Greene's Vietnam novel, *The Quiet American* (1956), does not deal explicitly with Catholic themes and although there is no overt Catholic milieu, I shall examine it in connection with the Catholic novels, because it has a religious theme. Greene is quoted as having said, "The novel was not political. It was, rather, religious (though not Catholic); it was a kind of morality about religion."[52] More accurately,

[50] These two statements of Mauriac's are quoted by Donat O'Donnell in *Maria Cross* (p. 25).

[51] *Woman of the Pharisees* (New York, Holt, 1946), p. 140.

[52] *New York Times*, January 20, 1957, Sec. 7, p. 8.

perhaps, it is a morality about irreligion: for the hero is an atheist who is no nearer to God at the end of the story than he is at the beginning. God and the ultimates burn in the background of *The Quiet American;* in the foreground blaze adultery and guilt. The fuel is much the same as it has been.

Yet despite Greene's disclaimer, *The Quiet American* is also a political novel. He is not consistent, having written to a friend: "I would say the theme of the book was religious as well as political."[53] The review that made the most of the novel's political implications was the one written by Robert G. Davis for the *New York Times Book Review.* Declaring *The Quiet American* to be "a political novel—or parable—about the war in Indochina,"[54] Mr. Davis deplored the anti-American bias displayed by the Englishman Fowler, the first-person narrator. Assuming that Fowler was Greene— because Fowler often quotes "almost verbatim from articles which Graham Greene wrote about Indochina for The London *Times* last spring"[55]—Mr. Davis implied that maybe Greene is really pink. Greene reacted with understandable indignation:

A good deal of misunderstanding is due to the apparent ignorance nowadays of a novelist's technique. More people should read Henry James' Prefaces and realize the importance of a point of view. If one uses the first person the point of view has obviously got to be I, and one must put one's self in I's skin as intensely as possible. It would be absurd, however, to imagine that the author is Fowler any more than he is the boy gangster in *Brighton Rock,* which was also told mainly through one point of view. As Pyle stood for complete engagement, Fowler obviously had to stand

[53] *New York Times*, August 26, 1956, Sec. 7, p. 8.
[54] *New York Times*, March 11, 1956, Sec. 7, p. 1.
[55] *Ibid.*, p. 32.

for an equally exaggerated viewpoint on the other side. Those who have read my war articles on Indochina will know that I am myself by no means a neutralist. I share certain of Fowler's views, but obviously not all of them—for instance, I don't happen to be an atheist. But even those views I share with Fowler I don't hold with Fowler's passion because I don't happen to have lost a girl to an American![56]

If you check the articles on Indochina which Mr. Davis mentioned, you will see that Greene does share some of Fowler's views but not all, and none of them with Fowler's intensity. On the other hand, Greene does not necessarily know more about his novel than Mr. Davis does. But a verdict in this matter is not of the utmost relevance. It is somewhat beside the point whether Greene is "I" or not. To show this let us, for the sake of argument, grant Mr. Davis' premise—that this book is riddled with political heresy. Even then his emphasis is unfortunate, since unhealthy political notions in themselves—whatever the critic's norm of healthiness—do not doom a novel, any more than healthy ones necessarily confer longevity on a novel. In the final analysis, only apolitical shortcomings are enough to bury a failing novel. Let us then enlarge our perspective by abandoning Greene's views on American foreign policy and turning our attention to literary issues.

Thomas Fowler, the cynical Englishman, and Alden Pyle, the naive American, seem to be perfect foils for each other. Fowler's story is the tragedy of a man who is unable to involve himself personally in human affairs; Pyle's is the tragedy of a man who gets too involved. Since Fowler's beliefs are always attended by procrastination, he rarely acts; since Pyle's beliefs are instantly translated into action, he is

[56] *New York Times*, August 26, 1956, Sec. 7, p. 8.

rarely quiet. (The title is obviously ironical.) Fowler's experience is his ruin: his experience has taught him to leave everything in the realm of chance and indecision. In doing so, he
connives at Pyle's death—reminiscent of Scobie's connivance
at the death of Ali. Pyle's innocence is his ruin: his innocence
has taught him to leave nothing in the sphere of caprice and
vacillation. In doing so, he hastens his own death.

Fowler represents experience in love and Europe in politics;
Pyle represents innocence in love and America in politics—
which, as one commentator points out,[57] is a typical Henry
James confrontation. Most un-Jamesian, however, is Greene's
condemnation of innocence. "Actually what Greene has done,"
as another commentator points out, "is to turn the Jamesian
theme of innocence versus experience inside out. Where
James sees this innocence as a redemptive quality that will
save the Old World, Greene sees it as positively ruinous in the
world of today."[58]

Despite Greene's ostensible partiality to Fowler, the latter's
policy of non-commitment is no more attractive to Greene
than is Pyle's indiscriminate commitment. Their differences
notwithstanding, Fowler and Pyle are failures for the same
reason: they are not informed by a religious conscience. In
Greene's eyes, this sterilizes their actions. When Fowler finally
does act—by acquiescing in the death of Pyle—he does not
act in terms of the right choice: his understanding is not
shored up by moral conviction. Since Pyle is nominally a
Unitarian, the religious and moral sense is not absent in him—
just quiescent, but it has the same effect on his conduct. It

[57] Donald Barr, Review of *The Quiet American*, in *Saturday
Review*, March 10, 1956, p. 12.
[58] Philip Rahv, "Wicked American Innocence," *Commentary*,
May 1956, p. 489.

prevents him from taking a detached view of the world, at the same time exhibiting a humane attachment to it. The most striking example of this flaw is the instance when Pyle looks down at the blood on his shoes, the freshly spattered blood of some women and children just killed by a bomb, and casually remarks, "I must get a shine before I see the Minister." Pyle is a missionary from what Greene calls "the graceless, sinless, empty chromium world."[59]

In an essay on François Mauriac, Greene bewails the disaster that overtook the English novel after the death of Henry James:

For with the death of James the religious sense was lost to the English novel, and with the religious sense went the sense of the importance of the human act. It was as if the world of fiction had lost a dimension: the characters of such distinguished writers as Mrs. Virginia Woolf and Mr. E. M. Forster wandered like cardboard symbols through a world that was paper-thin. Even in one of the most materialistic of our great novelists—in Trollope —we are aware of another world against which the actions of the characters are thrown into relief. The ungainly clergyman picking his black-booted way through the mud, handling so awkwardly his umbrella, speaking of his miserable income and stumbling through a proposal of marriage, exists in a way that Mrs. Woolf's Mr. Ramsay never does, because we are aware that he exists not only to the woman he is addressing but also in a God's eye. His unimportance in the world of the senses is only matched by his enormous importance in another world.[60]

The Quiet American is Greene's attempt to redirect our attention to the importance of the human act. In the words of Ralph Freedman, "*The Quiet American* is a work of art embodying

[59] *Another Mexico*, p. 226.
[60] *The Lost Childhood*, p. 69.

the principal failure of human involvement and choice in the twentieth century."[61] By contrast, how superficial and tiresome are those all too plentiful critics who, assuming that the sole interest and merit of *The Quiet American* lay in its political content, reduced it to a journalistic polemic, a topical tract. Misrouting attention from profound moral and religious issues, they obscured the fact that this novel—like most of Greene's mature novels as distinguished from his entertainments—reflects *la condition humaine*.

[61] "Novel of Contention: *The Quiet American*," *Western Review*, XXI (Autumn 1956), 81.

5 The Plays

GRAHAM GREENE's plays, like Henry James', are by-products of a novelist's career, with the difference that Greene's are relatively more successful on the stage than James' were. Still Greene's plays fall short of his best novels. *The Living Room*, Greene's first play, with Eric Portman as Father James Browne, was the sensation of the 1953 London season. Presented in New York the following year, with Walter Fitzgerald as the priest, it was a commercial failure. *The Potting Shed*, Greene's second play, had its world premiere in New York on January 29, 1957 at the Bijou Theatre, with Frank Conroy as Father William Callifer. Better received in New York than its predecessor, *The Potting Shed* is nonetheless artistically inferior to *The Living Room*. His third play, *The Complaisant Lover*, a London hit in 1959, moved to Broadway two years later with Michael Redgrave in the lead role. An urbane and amusing comedy about a domestic triangle, it is vastly different from the first two. His fourth and last play to date, *Carving a Statue*, starring Ralph Richardson, was first presented in London in 1964. Four years later, it was done in New York off-Broadway, a concession to the fact that it is the least of Greene's dramas.

My judgment as to the relative merit of these four plays is based upon having seen them as well as having

154

read them. My remarks, however, will be confined to the printed editions. I shall consider the first two plays together and at length, since they are similar and are the more formidable stage works. The latter two, since they are different from one another and from the preceding two, I shall treat separately towards the end of the chapter.

When a priest is a major character of Greene's, as he is in the two earlier plays and *The Power and the Glory,* he is invariably pivotal, the character on whom the plot turns; when priests are minor characters, as they are in *Brighton Rock, The Heart of the Matter, The End of the Affair,* and *A Burnt-Out Case,* they invariably influence the plot out of all proportion to the size of their roles. We need thus to examine the role played by the priest in Greene's Catholic works, with particular attention to Father Browne and Father Callifer.

Before we even adjust the focus of our microscope, we are struck by the fact that Greene has a very definite, and rather limited, concept of what a priest ought to be—a concept, by the way, often at variance with the accepted view. Holiness, piety, success, charm, self-esteem, community esteem, and even orthodoxy are not necessary planks in Greene's platform for the priesthood. On the other hand, belief in miracles and God's mercy, respect for human suffering, broad-mindedness, kindly tolerance, human warmth, and above all humility are necessary planks. These conclusions are inferred from a study of the many priests Greene admires, or at least sympathizes with, as well as the two he dislikes.

One priest who illustrates by default what Greene admires in a priest is Father Thomas in *A Burnt-Out Case.* He seeks a sign that God is pleased with him. He would welcome the grace of aridity, "walking in the footsteps of St. John of the Cross," and at the end, a spectacular martyrdom. Besides ascetical and self-sacrificial impulses motivated by ambition, there are other telltale signs of pride. He is scrupulous and condemns sinners. He is ambivalent about confidences. He longs to confide. But he is ashamed to admit a weakness, and there is the matter of finding a worthy confidante. When we recall Greene's well known aversion to theological proofs for the existence of God as a buttress to faith, we perceive another peccadillo. Doubting Father Thomas has a problem of faith which he blandly assumes can be cured by going over "the philosophical arguments."

Father Clay, in *The Heart of the Matter,* is the only other priestly creation Greene obviously dislikes. More complacent but less ambitious than Father Thomas, Father Clay loses no opportunity to contrast his virtues with the vices of others, walls up God's mercy, utters pious ejaculations, and adheres exclusively to the letter of the Church's teaching. It is important to understand the reason for Greene's vexation with Father Clay. It is not because sinlessness automatically evokes Greene's contempt, as John Atkins would have us believe. After all, Greene shows no intolerance towards Father Rank, the other priest in *The Heart of the Matter,* whose life is at least as irreproachable as Father Clay's. In fact Father Rank's humility has a far better claim to virtue than Father Clay's pride. No, Greene does not disapprove of Father Clay because he "omitted to sleep with someone else's wife,"[1] any more than he disapproves of Father Rank's celibacy.

None of Greene's priests—those he admires no more than

[1] John Atkins, *Graham Greene: A Biographical and Literary Study* (New York, Roy, 1957), p. 209.

the two he does not admire—believes it is possible to commit fornication or adultery and remain true to the spirit of morality. Nor are they indifferent to sins of the flesh. This is clear from the advice Father Browne gives Michael Dennis, the married psychologist, who is caught up in an illicit love affair with the priest's young niece, Rose Pemberton. "There's only one answer I can give. You're doing wrong to your wife, to Rose, to yourself—and to the God you don't believe in. Go away. Don't see her, don't write to her, don't answer her letters if she writes to you. She'll have a terrible few weeks. So will you. . . . We have to trust God." Moreover, Father Browne's solution is typical, echoing the advice of Father Crompton to Sarah and Father Rank to Scobie in similar situations. None of Greene's priests is guilty of the eighth capital sin: to deny sin where sin exists. In the words of Father Browne: "We [Catholics] do as many wrong things as you do, but we have the sense to know it."

In addition to this sense of sin, Greene's priests share a common attitude towards pain. Father Browne has enormous respect for human suffering, even for those, like Rose and Michael, who suffer in an unrighteous cause. In imputing much the same efficacy to unrighteous suffering as to righteous suffering, Father Browne is, of course, unorthodox, but at least he errs on the side of charity. Pain he considers inevitable. When Rose confronts her uncle with her dilemma—inability to bear the pain of separation if she gives Michael up; inability to bear the pain of Michael's wife if she runs off with him— he reminds her: "In a case like yours we always have to choose between suffering our own pain or suffering other people's. We can't *not* suffer." Pain he considers desirable, especially when it begets joy, as it often does. When Michael rages against the futility of Rose's death, Father Browne reminds him: "Suffering is a problem to us, but it doesn't seem a big problem to the woman when she has borne her child. Death is our child, we have to go through pain to bear our death. I'm crying out with the pain like you. But Rose—she's free, she's borne her child." A prevision of the way Father Browne and Michael meet and immediately part on the problem of pain is to be found in the conflict between the whisky priest and the Lieutenant. In the eyes of the latter, suffering is never desirable or even necessary; it is always wrong. But in the eyes of the whisky priest, "joy always depends on pain. Pain is part of joy. We are hungry and then think how we enjoy our food at last."

Greene's priests have complete trust in God's mercy, without forgetting St. Augustine's admonition: "Make neither of your own righteousness a safe-conduct to Heaven, nor of God's mercy a safe-conduct to sin."[2] Unlike his pharisaical sister Helen, who tries to make of her "own righteousness a safe-conduct to Heaven," Father Browne does not presumptuously anticipate the divine Judge's judgment on Rose, refuse her mercy, and rigidly apply pseudo-justice in order to condemn her. He believes no man is innocent enough to judge another, except on his knees; he acts on the words of St. Thomas Aquinas: "Mercy is more acceptable to God than sacrifice."[3] In like manner, the whisky priest puts all his hope in the mercy of God, in contrast to the nameless, self-righteous woman who puts all her hope in her own merits. At the other extreme, from these two pious, hypocritical women, with their proud disdain for appeals to mercy, is Padre José, that shepherd in the mist, who wrests sympathy from Greene solely be-

[2] Quoted by Dietrich von Hildebrand as the epigraph to *True Morality and Its Counterfeits*.
[3] *Summa Theologica* II-II, q. 30, a. 4.

cause he throws himself on divine mercy. "The mercies of the Lord I will sing forever," asserts the Psalmist (Ps. lxxxviii. 2). In this spirit, Father Rank bears the message of hope to Louise after Scobie's suicide, and following Pinkie's suicide, a nameless priest tells Rose no one can "conceive . . . the appalling strangeness of the mercy of God. . . . The Church does not demand that we believe any soul is cut off from mercy." In a 1953 interview, Greene revealed a single-minded intention in all his Catholic fiction: to show again and again the infinite mercy of God for the repentant sinner at the final hour.[4] Greene's arguments of hope are fleshed out in the persons of Father Browne and his fellow priests.

The prevalence of suicide among Greene's characters has caused a furor among certain critics. Elizabeth Sewell, for example, attributes to Greene an apotheosis of suicide which, she feels, amounts to a decadent inversion of life and death.[5] Sometimes, too, his priests are accused of being spokesmen for his allegedly too lenient attitude towards suicide. Father Browne and Father Rank dissent from the opinion of the other characters that Rose and Scobie are necessarily damned. The former tells Michael, "Nobody claims we can know what she thought at the end. Only God was with her at the end." The latter tells Mrs. Scobie, "The Church knows all the rules. But it doesn't know what goes on in a single human heart." Greene's priests paraphrase a quotation beloved by Pinkie— who tries to make "of God's mercy a safe-conduct to sin": "Between the stirrup and the ground, he something sought and something found." Somewhat in the nature of a discursive explanation of this is the answer Greene once made to those

---

[4] Martin Shuttleworth and Simon Raven, "The Art of Fiction III: Graham Greene," *Paris Review*, I (Autumn 1953), 31.

[5] Sewell, *op. cit.*, p. 57.

who are shocked at his suicide motif. In an interview with Henry Hewes, he said: "Of course, suicide is a mortal sin. But who is to say that a person committing suicide is in a *state* of mortal sin just because he dies without having confessed his mortal sin?"[6]

Suicide brings us to Father William Callifer. An attempted suicide by his nephew, James Callifer, when he was fourteen years old, has blighted both their lives. This incident, which occurred thirty years before *The Potting Shed* opens, resulted from the confusion begot in the sensitive boy's mind by his uncle's devout Catholicism and his father's crusading atheism. "He took everything I told you," Father Callifer relates to James, "and made fun of it. He made me a laughing stock before you. I had taught you about the Virgin birth and he cured you with physiology." After hanging himself in a fit of despair in a potting shed on his father's estate, James is found by Father Callifer who, on account of his love for the boy, enters into a terrible bargain with God. He entreats the Almighty: "Take away my faith, but let him live." This love-inspired willingness to barter with God is yet another characteristic of Greene's priests. The whisky priest offers to undergo eternal damnation in exchange for the salvation of his corrupt natural daughter: "Oh God," he prays, "help her. Damn me. I deserve it, but let her live forever." To realize that this offering of self-damnation is not peculiar to Greene's priests, however, we have only to recall the example of Scobie.

Refusing to limit their knowledge to the evidence of their senses, Greene's priests believe in miracles. Unlike Father Callifer's brother, H. C., who "stands," as Greene said to Hewes, "for 'a whole crowd of dull dogs' of which H. G.

[6] Henry Hewes, "Resurrection Will Out," *Saturday Review*, February 16, 1957, p. 27.

Wells was perhaps the most famous," they are never material-
ists or rationalists. Father Crompton, in *The End of the Affair*,
with his insistence that it is more sensible to believe that
anything may happen than it is to restrict the possible, is
typical, as is the whisky priest who bases his belief in miracles
on faith—"faith in the spittle that healed the blind man and
the voice that raised the dead."

In this respect Father Callifer in *The Potting Shed* is not
typical, by any means; he spends half his life disbelieving in
miracles: belief in the miraculous characterizes his life prior to
ordination and the first and last years of his priestly career.
His disbelief in the interim can be traced to his misunderstanding of the events in the potting shed. When he tenders what
he loves most to God, he mistakenly assumes that the offer is
accepted: he assumes that God by destroying his faith restores
James to life. Feeling as he does, his belief in God naturally
withers—although there is much evidence to show that it never
dies—since he is tormented by the question, what kind of a
miracle is it that diminishes faith? When James at long last
furnishes him with a clue to what actually happened, his
question lapses into irrelevancy and his dormant faith leaps up.
Let Greene himself tell us what the clue is: "The priest's offer
to give up his faith in return for his young nephew's life is 'a
contract made in the dark.' When the boy lives, the priest
only imagines that God has accepted his offer. But faith is 'a
gift from God, not a merit, and therefore was not his to give
away,' as is proved when he recovers faith."[7]

With the two indicated exceptions, Greene's priests do not

[7] "A Spiritual Suspense Story," *Life*, April 1, 1957, p. 68. Most
commentators stumbled on this point. Mary McCarthy, for example, reviewing the play for *Partisan Review*—XXIV (Spring
1957), 272—assumed that God has accepted the priest's offer, and
thus she declared the whole affair of the miracle to be fraudulent.

think highly of themselves. Believing he has lost his faith, Father Callifer feels he is of no use to anyone, but still he says Mass, hears confessions, and visits the sick faithfully. Father Browne also accuses himself of failure; he blames himself for failing his niece. But is he not too hard on himself? Considering his office and his person, what counsel could he, whose "tongue is heavy with the Penny Catechism," give, other than that which he does give—separation and prayer? Rose knows this: she knows that only by renouncing her life of sin and returning to God can she find peace. But she does not want peace at this price, and thus she fails herself. Father Rank, like Father Browne, has an unjustified feeling of futility. Before Scobie, he berates himself: "They send for me when they are dying. . . . I've never been any good to the living." But judging from the consolation he gives Mrs. Scobie, after her husband's suicide, his self-deprecation is as unwarranted, or at least as excessive, as Father Browne's. Where charity is concerned, Greene's priests are most painfully aware of their defections from the ideal of Christ.

The other characters of Greene do not think highly of his priests, either. As we have seen, the bibulous priest, in *The Power and the Glory*, is branded a "whisky priest." Father Browne has to smart under Helen's taunt: "Oh, the Church is well rid of a useless priest like you, James." And the only person who stands between Father Callifer and a complaint by his parishioners on his lax conduct to the Bishop is his devoted housekeeper. No one snips the tassels from their cassock sashes to serve as the relics of a saint. Perhaps Greene has never limned a priest whose coat buttons are snatched, because Greene wishes to dramatize the fact that Christ made salvation in His Church depend primarily on the Mass, the sacraments, and the liturgical functions administered by priests, not primarily on the holiness or lack of holiness of His priests. The Church never guarantees that her priests will be saints. She does guarantee that when a priest baptizes, absolves from sin, or administers the Holy Eucharist, it is Christ Who is acting: "*I* baptize thee," "*I* absolve thee," "This is *My* Body; This is *My* Blood." Whatever faults Greene's priests have, the power of Christ still works in them. Consequently, their dignity is not necessarily linked with personal holiness.

Whatever common characteristics Greene's priests possess —and I have not attempted to note all of them—they are never caricatures. They are rare in the contemporary theatre, because Greene recognizes the man beneath the priest, as most other playwrights (Paul Vincent Carroll and G. B. Shaw, in *Saint Joan*, are exceptions) do not. The tragedy of Father Browne is ultimately the tragedy of a man who is not a saint, just as Othello is the tragedy of a jealous man, not a soldier. Greene refuses to subscribe to the stereotype of the clergyman—a holier-than-thou, self-righteous, hypocritical, too easily intimidated buffoon—perpetuated by J. M. Synge, Marcel Aymé, Tennessee Williams, G. B. Shaw (excluding *Saint Joan*), and many others. The spectacle of the same old clerical shape filched out of the stencil pile gets a little tiresome. Besides, it is difficult to understand why the clergyman alone is exempt from what Edmund Fuller calls the "new compassion" which, in essence, amounts to a perverse romanticizing of "the genial rapist, the jolly slasher, the fun-loving dope pusher."[8] Inasmuch as the sympathy of most contemporary playwrights is vast enough to make them hug these characters to their hearts, it is all the more startling that they should balk at ever creating a credible clergyman, let alone idealizing one.

I hope it is clear that I am not suggesting that art should

[8] *Man in Modern Fiction* (New York, Random, 1958), p. 33.

serve propaganda ends, that any playwright should plump for the Catholic priesthood or the Protestant ministry. Nor do I suggest that any playwright should feel obliged to depict a particular priest or a particular minister in a favorable light. When I consider the treatment of the priest in Marcel Aymé's *Clerambard*, for example, it is exclusively on artistic grounds. He is there merely to be the butt of the other characters' jibes and to provide comic relief for the audience. In short he is a caricature: no attempt has been made to get inside him and flesh him out as a recognizable human being, with some of the foibles human beings are subject to. How different is Greene's practice: even his two unsympathetic priests come off as rounded, believable characters. Although the tendency to parody the clergyman, in a superficial way, is also a staple of the modern novel, this tendency is less widespread. Here Greene's attempt to fashion priests who are capable of working on the emotions finds its counterpart in the work of Mauriac, Bernanos, and Alan Paton, as well as some others.

At the outset of this chapter, I declared my preference for *The Living Room* as the superior work of art. Since the New York drama critics were unanimous in preferring *The Potting Shed*, my greater enthusiasm for the first of Greene's plays puts me in a lonely minority. To support my dissenting judgment, I shall have to express an opinion on matters other than major characters. *The Potting Shed* strikes me as inferior for three reasons. To begin with, the minor characters in *The Potting Shed* are less solid than their forebears in *The Living Room*. At least two of the characters in the more recent play are there merely to tell the audience something rather than to do something on stage. Mrs. Potter appears solely to explain something of what happened in the potting shed; Miss Connolly appears solely to explain what sort of life Father Callifer has led. After they illuminate the past and the plot no longer needs them, in the manner of skywriting they evaporate. Closely related to this is the impression that one or two other minor characters, such as Corner and John Callifer, are on stage just to swell the cast—the play would be no different for their absence. And the whole family of earnest unbelievers is drawn with an exaggeration that makes them slightly implausible. No such character imperfections blemish *The Living Room*.

The Potting Shed is neither fish nor fowl. Greene does not divide his plays, as he does his novels, into serious works and entertainments. It is just as well, for if he did *The Potting Shed* would defy classification. For the first time in his fictional output, he tries to blend a suspense story, featuring a secret carefully withheld until the right psychological moment, with his traditional Catholic themes. The two do not mix, at least as stirred by Greene. Here the particular suspense story format —the what-done-it trek backward from an effect to a cause— is a blind alley leading him away from the heart of the matter, the miracle. *The Potting Shed* leaves unanswered the nature of the all-important relationship between the miracle and Father Callifer's loss of faith: this relationship is so nebulous that no amount of careful reading can pin it down. As we have seen, the answer is finally supplied by Greene in an interview granted to a reporter for *Life*. But this is hardly satisfactory; it is the business of the playwright to create in the play all the effects that pertain thereto. When the reader is forced to rely on program notes provided by the author for the correct interpretation, then the play is not much of a success. Greene's admission, following his explanation, that his point may not have been made too clearly in the play can be taken as a sign that he is aware of his lack of craftmanship here.

By comparison with *The Potting Shed*, whatever faults may be charged to *The Living Room* are venial—the New York drama critics notwithstanding. Oddly enough, their unanimously unfavorable reviews of *The Living Room* were based almost exclusively on the outlook of the play, rather than on the play itself. "Graham Greene can certainly make religion sound difficult,"[9] Brooks Atkinson was moved to observe in his notice on *The Living Room*. After praising Atkinson's observation, a reviewer for *Theatre Arts* added, "In *The Potting Shed* religion sounds much less difficult."[10] And a reviewer for *Time* wrote that "*The Potting Shed* is much less dour than *The Living Room*."[11] Implicit in these judgments is a pseudo-syllogism:

> Only a play that expresses faith in God simply and joyfully can be considered a sound religious drama.
>
> *The Living Room* does not express faith in God simply and joyfully.
>
> Ergo *The Living Room* cannot be considered a sound religious drama.

Remembering Aeschylus and Sophocles, Dostoyevsky and Undset, and, for that matter, a sizeable portion of the Bible, particularly Job and St. Paul, one can only wonder whether this shortsighted presumption rises even to the level of man thinking, let alone to the level of serious criticism. A play ought to be reviewed as a play, according to dramatic standards, and

[9] *New York Times*, November 18, 1954, p. 40.
[10] *Theatre Arts*, April 1957, p. 15.
[11] *Time*, February 11, 1957, p. 70.

not as an act of religious faith. It is a shame that lovers of serious drama in New York were discouraged from attending a powerfully gripping play, rich in human emotion, by such sophomoric provincialism.

By his own admission, Greene prefers play writing to motion picture writing, "mainly because revisions in the theatre come about through seeing that something you've written does not work rather than because of someone's opinion in a story conference."[12] And he enjoys writing plays at least as much as he enjoys writing novels[13]—as Chekhov once remarked: "The novel is a lawful wife, but the stage is a noisy, flashy mistress"[14]—even though he realizes how far he is from displaying a theatrecraft as masterful as his novelcraft. "I'm not loosened up yet," he says. "And I don't take sufficient advantage of the director's technique."[15] In addition, both plays betray Greene's brief familiarity with the ways of the theatre. *The Potting Shed* sputters at the start. Greene the novelist could ignite in the initial chapter what Greene the playwright takes a whole act to do. Ideological combat, present to a greater degree than in any of the novels, threatens to overwhelm *The Living Room*. But the storytelling and the writing, both naturally brilliant, shine through the technical flaws, particularly in *The Living Room*.

François Mauriac was a stranger to the theatre until he was fifty years old; Greene remained a stranger until he was forty-nine. This is the first in a series of amazing parallels between Greene's transfer to the theatre and Mauriac's. A novelist has

[12] Hewes, *op. cit.*, p. 26.
[13] Cf. Greene's introduction to *The Potting Shed*, printed in the Bijou Theatre playbill.
[14] Quoted by Brooks Atkinson from a letter by Chekhov.
[15] Hewes, *op. cit.*, p. 26.

to work alone, Greene muses in the program introduction to *The Potting Shed*, but the theatre delights him because it is a group enterprise. Recalling the circumstances of his second play, *Les Mal-Aimés*, Mauriac writes: "I will always remember the rehearsals in a corner of the unheated foyer of the Comédie Française, in bitter cold, the actors bundled up to their ears in coats and mufflers."[16] Recognizing the fact that the stage requires a special technique, neither has hesitated to put himself to school to the director. As Henry James learned before them, turning to the stage in the midst of a busy career as a novelist can be hazardous. Unreasonable critics expect too much versatility of novelists turned dramatists: they expect an equivalent command of the theatre medium. From coming late to the theatre, Mauriac and Greene have written plays that suffer in form from a novelist's conditioning. *Asmodée* and *The Living Room* totter on the brink of prolixity, a depth that only the novelist has the leisure to explore.

The best plays of Mauriac and Greene, in my judgment at least, are their first plays. Both *Asmodée* and *The Living Room* feature important characters who are unconscious hypocrites, people who act in good faith and do not realize they are impostors. The language Mauriac employs to describe the hero of *Asmodée* is as much a description of Aunt Helen as it is of Blaise Couture. "The hero of *Asmodée* is not aware of the fact that he is deceiving the people around him. When he speaks of his conscience he believes he is acting in accordance with its dictates. He is impelled by a passion for dominating people, for possessing them. ... He is obviously the Pharisee par excellence."[17] M. Couture and Aunt Helen identify their cause with God's cause; revel in their imaginary freedom from

[16] *New York Times*, March 23, 1958, Sec. 2, p. 3.
[17] *Ibid.*

sin, never permitting the moral frailty of others to remind them of their own; induce others—to whom they feel morally superior—to do evil to attain their selfish ends; experience no sense of guilt; and are continually scandalized by the sins of others, gloat over them, and enjoy condemning them.

Until his recent death, Paul Claudel was the high priest among contemporary Catholic dramatists. When Greene's dramas are compared with Claudel's, we are immediately struck with the differences between them rather than the similarities. Even though Greene, like Claudel, chooses to dramatize crucial moments in the spiritual evolution of his characters, his settings are vastly different. Claudel specialized in historical plays set in the Napoleonic era, Renaissance Europe, or medieval France. A more fundamental difference arises from the divergent functions Claudel and Greene ascribe to the theatre. Whereas Claudel's plays usually have a propaganda aim, Greene's plays are largely free of propaganda. Whereas the catechetical labors of Claudel's characters sometimes get in the way of their animation, Greene's plays fairly crackle with dramatic tension engendered by vitally charged characters.

Adulterous love and unhappy love are trademarks of Claudel as much as they are Greene's. But Greene never leaves us, as Claudel does, with the uncomfortable feeling that the ultimate villain is God. "Love in Claudel," remarks Martin Turnell, "is of its nature unhappy. . . . We have the impression that the lovers are unhappy in their love because God intends them to be unhappy, that God is engaged in a cat-and-mouse game with His creatures, dashing the cup from their lips at the very moment when the obstacles to happiness and a Christian life have been removed."[18] Greene's God has more

[18] "Claudel: The Intolerance of Genius," *Commonweal*, May 27, 1955, p. 206.

in common with the Christian God of the New Testament than with this "tribal god of the Old."[19]

Jibes at notorious unbelievers are to be found in the works of both writers. Claudel's passionate denunciations of Gide, Renan, and Zola are far better known than Greene's less direct and more temperate attacks on H. G. Wells and Bertrand Russell in *The Potting Shed*. But Greene, unlike Claudel, has never allowed his allegiance to Catholicism to magnify his appreciation of Catholic literary figures. G. K. Chesterton and Hilaire Belloc are cases in point: Greene, leaning over backwards to avoid the charge that he patronizes members of the same club, does less than justice to "The Chesterbelloc,"[20] whereas Claudel accords them more than their due. Furthermore, Claudel's excessive zeal for Coventry Patmore contrasts starkly with Greene's harsh strictures on Léon Bloy and Eric Gill.[21] Perhaps this is Greene's way of overcompensating for the evident distaste he attaches to plainly partisan literary criticism.

"This is an odd play," comments John Chapman on *The Potting Shed*, "perhaps a Roman Catholic version of T. S. Eliot's peculiarly fascinating and Episcopal *The Cocktail Party*."[22] That the comparison should come to mind is not at all strange; the two plays have much in common. Both plays open with drawing room chitchat, which is nonetheless deeply revelatory of character, and close on a letdown. In both, the preliminary scenes lay the ground-work for the dramatic decisions that will be made later. Questing for peace of soul,

[19] *Ibid.*

[20] Review of Hilaire Belloc's *On the Place of Gilbert Chesterton in English Letters, Spectator,* October 11, 1940, p. 370. See also "A Visit to Morin."

[21] *The Lost Childhood,* pp. 77-79; 132-135.

[22] New York *Daily News,* January 30, 1957, p. 52.

the two protagonists, Celia Copleston and James Callifer, turn first to psychiatry and then to religion before they achieve the desired serenity. Rigid characters are skillfully juxtaposed with flexible ones in *The Cocktail Party* and *The Potting Shed*. Eliot contrasts the pedestrian lives of Lavinia and Edward with the spectacular sanctity of Celia: Lavinia and Edward are only capable of resignation; Celia is capable of martyrdom. Greene tends to do the same thing when he contrasts James' giant step from utter spiritual vacuity to faith with his mother's pygmy step from atheism to agnosticism—heralded by the assertion: "We are none of us sure. When you aren't sure you are alive."

The Living Room also has affinities with *The Cocktail Party*. In part, these plays are debates in dialogue, in an esthetically communicated form, of the relative virtues between religion and psychiatry, with the difference that Henry Harcourt Reilly combines the office of priest and psychiatrist in *The Cocktail Party*, whereas in *The Living Room* there is a *vis-à-vis* confrontation between the two. Ponderous and dull in the hands of lesser craftsmen, these intellectual exchanges are made exciting by Eliot and Greene. The latter especially knows the trick of making the friction of ideas as exciting as a waterfront brawl. The ultimate impact of these plays lies in the ability of their authors to wear their art on the sleeves of their hair shirts. These plays do not express hopelessness, despite the despair felt by one or two characters, nor are they "Destitute of love for human kind . . . as ferocious as Cotton Mather";[23] on the contrary, in the end they express hope everlasting, life triumphing over death, and illustrate—*The Cocktail Party* literally—that beautiful *pensée* of Mauriac's:

[23] Brooks Atkinson, Review of *The Living Room*, in the *New York Times*, November 21, 1954, Sec. 2, p. 1.

"Each one of us is more crucified than he knows. If you search each man for the cross which is part of his destiny, you will always end by finding it. In each of us, a cross grows as we grow, and to be stretched on it before our last breath, either voluntarily or by force, means our salvation."[24]

II

The very title of Greene's next play, *The Complaisant Lover,* posed a problem. When Irene Selznick, the American producer, brought the London hit comedy to Broadway in 1961, she wondered if the word "complaisant" might not strike American audiences as too highbrow and suggested substituting the word "complacent." According to a letter Mrs. Selznick received from the author, this was out of the question. His play, concerned with two men who share the one's wife, is very specifically about complaisance, not complacency.

In English, the word 'complaisant' when attached to a husband has had one meaning and one meaning only, as in French: that is to say a husband who is prepared to keep his wife by allowing her full liberty of action. For this reason using this adjective with the title of lover makes it quite certain for an English public that a sexual connotation is given to the word. On the other hand complacent calls first to mind the dull and uninteresting meaning, 'self-satisfied.'

[24] *The Stumbling Block* (New York, Philosophical Library, 1952), p. 10.

The adjective in the title as Greene's firm letter makes clear, incidentally, applies as much to the husband as to the lover. The play bears this out. For when the lover reproaches the husband with the words: "You can be a complaisant husband if you like, I'm not going to be a complaisant lover," the husband retorts: "The two are inseparable."

So understood, the title serves as a warning that Greene is departing, at least to an extent, from the serious mood of *The Living Room* and *The Potting Shed* to compose a new kind of sophisticated divertissement. For *The Complaisant Lover* is related to the earlier two dramas much as the last two entertainments are related to the works that preceded them. The self-parody, subdued in *Loser Takes All* but so marked in *Our Man in Havana,* recurs here. Whereas previously in the novels and plays, Greene has always treated adultery with sobriety, he now turns infidelity into a farce. "Please, not before Christmas!" the passionate but proper wife, Mary Rhodes, begs her improbable lover, Clive Root, a bookseller who is not interested in lust, as he barely summons the courage to ask her to run off with him. (There is an order to these things: Christmas first; concupiscence later.) But if the lovers are unlike Greene's previous lovers, the husband, Victor Rhodes, a passionless dentist overly given to practical jokes, is even more unpredictable. When he makes the distressing discovery that he is being cuckolded, his reaction seems all wrong or at least unexpectedly generous: he modestly proposes that he retain his wife during the week but that she be free to weekend with her lover.

Greene is writing a self-styled "French farce" here which also departs from that tradition in certain ways.

As Walter Kerr puts it: "Whereas every dramatist of adultery from early French folk farce onward has always started out by supposing that the idyll would be a jolly one if only it weren't for all those intrusive bellhops, outraged husbands, suddenly opened doors, and so forth, Mr. Greene acknowledges the peppery existence of bellhops, husbands, and doors but refuses to blame them for a single thing."[25] In the standard triangular comedy, neither the cuckold nor the adulterer is voluntarily complaisant where his rival is concerned. In the standard sex comedy, the lover is a Casanova, but not Clive. He is a sensualist-with-scruples, so that despite his success in leading a succession of restless middle-class wives into adultery, he remains an unconvincing seducer.

And as Richard Gilman points out: "It is a play, moreover, wherein the element of choice, so basic to the genre, becomes painful rather than liberating, the very intolerability of the necessity to choose constituting the substance and tension of the drama."[26] This is Mary's dilemma. "I don't know, I don't want to choose," she tells her husband after what has been going on is finally rubbed under his nose. "I don't want to leave you and the children. I don't want to leave him. Victor, dear Victor, why can't we sometimes, just once, have our cake and eat it?" But her plight is an enviable one. Both men gallantly concede that she should have her cake and eat it, too. She becomes the winner who takes all: she has the security of marriage and the excitement of sex. And so the play is no more a typical bedroom farce than it is a typical adultery in Greeneland.

[25]Review of *The Complaisant Lover,* in the *New York Herald Tribune,* November 2, 1961.

[26]Review of *The Complaisant Lover,* in *Commonweal,* November 24, 1961, p. 233.

Still *The Complaisant Lover* is intended as an amalgam of extremes, farce and tragedy. Conventional farce is present in the basic situation — a bored wife duping an obtuse husband by taking a lover — in the lover's preference for other men's wives, and in the highjinks attendant upon the discovery scene. In addition, farce is present in Victor's nocturnal precautions in locking up everything in his house *except* his wife. The makings of tragedy lurk in such sober epigrams as the following, "Love's painful at any age" (Mary) . "What liars and cheats love makes of us" (Clive) . "The good are horribly hard to leave" (Mary). In addition, near-tragedy lurks in Victor's passing reaction to the news. He tells his wife that he repaired to the garage where he contemplated suicide by carbon monoxide poisoning.

The alliance of levity and seriousness is never wholly successful unless there is equilibrium. But in this play light-heartedness overwhelms solemnity. The usual ploys of straightforward adultery — the insinuation that Clive is a casual acquaintance and the brief afternoon encounters looking forward to a clandestine weekend in a foreign capital — are routed by a multitude of comical caprices. This is so, because the craftsmanship is weighted on the side of farce. The rich farcical impact depends upon the imaginative pictures and patterns evoked by dramatized incidents. The tragical impact is almost non-existent, since it depends upon direct telling without a detour through the imagination.

It is instructive to see how much more effectively someone like T. S. Eliot in "Sweeney Erect", for example, combines the two genres. By obtaining artistic balance between levity and seriousness, Eliot wrests a resonant comic tone from tragic substance, whereas Greene must be content with superimposing a feeble tragic tone on farcical substance. Despite his inability to retain control of his disparate materials, however, there is much that is rewarding here: the sophisticated badinage, the swift evocation of an appealing mood, and especially the zany Marx Brothers scene in an Amsterdam hotel room.

III

Carving a Statue concerns a mediocre sculptor, identified only as the "father," who is carving a thirty foot statue of God the Father — after his own image — on which he has been working for fifteen years. His motherless son, "fifteen or sixteen," identified only as the "boy," frantically tries to get his father's attention, but the father is exclusively interested in his own work. Desperate for affection, the boy brings home a girl, identified only as the "first girl," when he believes his father is away drunk. But the father returns, sends the boy on an errand, and seduces the girl in his toolshed.

In the last act, the boy has a new girl friend, identified only as the "second girl." She is deaf and dumb. They are planning to run away from his unresponsive father and get married. Again the boy, who throughout is represented as uncommonly simple, is frustrated: this time by the family doctor, Dr. Parker, the sole character in the play who is provided with a name. A notorious lecher, he lures the girl into another room and so frightens her by his advances that she rushes out of the studio into the street and into the path of an oncoming car. She is run over and killed. The boy is desolated. Even then the father withholds rapport until the boy threatens to hang himself from the statue. "Come down. It's not too late for you and me," he whimpers repentantly. But it is too late, for no sooner does the boy come down than the *idée fixe* returns in a new guise. The father declares that he has been mistaken: the statue is not of God but of Lucifer. And just before the curtain descends, he resolves to throw himself into the newly conceived work with greater intensity than ever.

Carving a Statue is swamped by murky symbolism — abetted by the nameless characters — having something to do with this association of ideas: just as God the Father willed His Son to die, so the sculptor demands a sacrifice of his son. And the end of the play is related to this: what kind of a God would willingly allow His Son to die? "It's not God the Father," muses the sculptor, looking at the statue. "I know that now. No love or tenderness there. Only pride. Like Lucifer's." Whatever the symbolism may be, this is Greene's most Manichaean work, unrelieved by allusions to divine grace and mercy. It is especially puzzling coming in the wake of two sportive entertainments and a play and directly preceding two optimistic novels. And whatever the reason for vinegar in the midst of honey, my impression is that this is not only the least of Greene's dramas, but it is perhaps the least of all his works.

In a preface to the play, which he revealingly calls "Epitaph for a Play," Greene states that his intention was to fashion a character based on Benjamin Robert Haydon, who was obsessed — to the sacrifice of any personal life — by the desire to do great Biblical subjects, already, even in his day, out of fashion. You cannot read the diaries of Haydon without realizing that he had a true daemon and yet he had no talent at all — surely a farcical character, though he came to a tragic end. In my story, as I intended it, the artist lost even his tragic end — no Tom Thumb was capable of shattering permanently his dream and driving him to the saving bullet. He had a greater capacity to recover than poor Haydon.

My judgment that this is Greene's biggest failure is based largely on the contention that the completed play realizes so little of the avowed intention. I view the self-absorbed sculptor — little like Haydon — as a genuinely evil man, not a fool out of farce. He is utterly indifferent to human suffering, except as it touches himself. He uses his work to "hold the pain of the world away from me." He is utterly indifferent to people, except as subjects for the artist to use. And he justifies all this by smearing God; yet pretending to take his cue from Him as exemplified by this exchange at the close of the second act:

FATHER: I don't have to worry about love. God doesn't love . . . He's an artist. He doesn't love.
BOY: Did He hate his son?
FATHER: He didn't love or hate him. He used him as a subject. That's what the Son was for.

I fail to see *Carving a Statue* as "a game played with the same extremes of mood as *The Complaisant Lover*." But then I suspect that for all his brave declaration of intent, Greene too had his doubts, for he confesses: "This play was never fun."

6 The Later Novels

I

THE MATURE novels of Graham Greene fall into two categories: the Catholic novels, which I discussed in chapter four, and the post-Catholic novels, to be treated here. The division, to be sure, is somewhat arbitrary. *The Quiet American* and *A Burnt-Out Case* (1961) are transitional books: they straddle the two categories. They are less Catholic novels than religious ones. What an anonymous reviewer of *A Burnt-Out Case* says of that book, in this connection, has comparable validity for *The Quiet American*. "Here moral questions do not depend on such local beliefs as the sin of taking the sacrament with a lie withheld from confession, but rather on such questions as must be asked by all, Catholics and atheists alike, who cannot but consider those questions to which orthodox religions proffer answers."[1] My solution is to handle the earlier one in chapter four and the later one here. The alternative to devote a separate chapter to the two, the religious novels, would necessitate a further chapter devoted to *The Comedians* (1966) and *Travels with My Aunt* (1970), the black humor novels. But this would be unfortunate, since there is some, if less, religious concern in the two most recent novels, as well as glimpses of black comedy in the so-called religious novels. The proliferation of skimpy chapters and misleading titles can be avoided by doing the three latest ones together under the heading, the later novels.

[1] *London Times Literary Supplement,* January 20, 1961.

In *The Heart of the Matter,* Greene created a character who is too caught up in human affairs. In *A Burnt-Out Case,*[2] he creates a character who tries to resign from life. The road Scobie takes is paved with good intentions: he would manage the affairs of those around him to their advantage. What can be said of Scobie, and for that matter the road to hell, is more than can be predicated of Querry: he is without intentions, good or evil, and has little concern for himself or others. It is curious that Querry, not Scobie, should strive for detachment. After all, Querry's attachments, unlike Scobie's, had been more painful for others than for himself. And he did not seem to mind visiting pain on outsiders.

As the latter story opens, Querry, a spiritually burnt-out case smarting from emotional torpor, is en-route incognito to a remote leproserie, run by missionaries, in the Belgian Congo, where he plans to lose touch with the human condition. He aspires to the condition of a Hollow Man, hoping simply to go out with a whimper. (Ironically, though, his world ends with a bang.) He has no interest in anything: He has lapsed from fame (a world-famous European architect), women (a wife and a succession of mistresses) , and religion (Roman Catholicism) . Yet at the leproserie, something of life stubbornly persists in tugging at Querry. He succeeds in putting an end to his profession, fear, and the desire to sleep with a woman;

[2]Part of this consideration of *A Burnt-Out Case* first appeared in substantially different form — for I am convinced that my view of it then was short-sighted — in *Renascence,* Autumn 1961, pp. 48-49.

but he cannot entirely disengage himself from laughter, suffering, feeling, and the desire to be of use.

In the Greene canon, Querry's prototype is Fowler, the *disengagé* Englishman, in *The Quiet American*. They are vacant protagonists, drained of emotion, seeking refuge in passivity — Querry by choice; Fowler through events not altogether in his control. They both have roots in Conrad's Heyst, the modern progenitor of characters who fail in human involvement, although Querry is ultimately more Heystian by reason of his near-recovery. But common to all three novels, and others with similar characters who withdraw from the world, is the inability to rise to the heights of dramatic intensity. This is the inevitable consequence whenever emphasis is placed on intra-character conflict rather than inter-character conflict. Other characters lurk in the background, but Querry's refusal to become involved with them emotionally, to the point of love or hate, does not enhance the work dramatically.

However, the meticulous attention that Greene pays to maintaining and heightening suspense throughout *A Burnt-Out Case* dwarfs this built-in limitation. Always a master of suspenseful story-telling, Greene outdoes himself here. The reason why Querry is an empty man is shrouded in one kind of suspense until the appearance of Parkinson, a gutter-journalist, halfway through the novel. Prior to his arrival, the reader is left to guess at the reason for Querry's spiritual mutilation. Is his emptiness aridity, the dark night of the soul which is a grace and a state of prayer, as Rycker and Father Thomas, the two most scrupulous characters, allege? Or is it corruption?

At the instigation of Rycker, a sanctimonious planta-
tion owner, Parkinson, with a nose for good copy, has
come to present Querry to the world as a saint with a
past, "atoning for a reckless youth by serving others."
Rycker and Father Thomas are hopeful that the interview
will establish Querry as a combination St. Augustine-Dr.
Schweitzer. But Querry is uncooperative. By confessing
a litany of contagions, past and present, he *appears* to
torpedo the attempt to canonize him. A *superficial* reading would have it that the interview establishes Querry's
status, beyond doubt. He is not *"the* Querry"; he is a
man facing the void, by his own admission, believing in
nothing at all. The result of Parkinson's visit is that
the suspense is blown up and the reader's interest is shipwrecked.

This is not the case at all. A *profound* reading shows
that far from weakening the novel, *A Burnt-Out Case* is
actually strengthened by the confession of moral bank-
ruptcy. It only destroys what is a source of suspense — Is
Querry a despondent saint or a cold blooded bastard? —
for the two least sympathetic characters, Rycker and
Father Thomas. At the same time, the confession leaves
intact the real suspense: will this burnt-out case succeed
in rekindling "feeling" in his heart? Besides Querry may
be deprecating himself, lying, in order to work out his
recovery away from the glare of publicity. The real suspense, cogent and impressive, is intensified by the interview. It does not dismiss the ambiguous note in Querry's
character, but it does provoke the mature reader to
dismiss the unrealistic either-or way of defining Querry.
At the same time, the interview deepens the ambiguity by

subordinating the character cleft to the ultimate issue: can he come back?

Although *A Burnt-Out Case* is full of character gems, excellent descriptions, brilliant similies, thought-provoking epigrammatic observations, and dialogues as dramatic as the pistol shots that provide the finale, little attempt is made to rival the richness of detail and the unique feel of foreign places that make Greene's earlier novels so memorable. But far from a cause for regret, this muted quality works to the advantage of the novel. The relative lack of interest in detail and locale is functional: the protagonist's detachment and fatigue are meant to sag through the whole novel. For example, there is a description of the river bank across from the mission house. "On the other shore the great trees, with roots above the ground like the ribs of a half-built ship, stood out over the green jungle wall, brown at the top like stale cauliflowers." This is typical: the vegetation is "brown" and has gone "stale," like the protagonist and the poor suffering human flesh of the lepers. There is no discrepancy between what Querry is and does, and where he is. A burnt-out case inhabits a burnt-out place.

The alternative, to assume that Greene's erstwhile descriptive prowess has simply deserted him, is untenable. A glance at the two African journals which comprise *In Search of a Character* will dispel this. Originally not intended for publication, the journal of his trip to the Belgian Congo in 1959 was the raw material for the novel that became *A Burnt-Out Case*. A shorter journal, of a wartime convoy to West Africa in 1941, was a prelude to the writing of *The Heart of the Matter*. The point is that when we compare the recorded impressions of the tropical landscape in both, we perceive no diminution in spirited, colorful writing. In the more recently written novel, then, Greene has deliberately chosen a subdued manner to suit the subdued matter.

A Burnt-Out Case is the last of Greene's better novels. In the two that follow, *The Comedians* and *Travels with My Aunt*, he ceases to do what he does best. He calls a halt to the agonizingly and eloquently mounted lifelong tussle with the Almighty. In lieu of probing the mysteries of human life, posing some of the stickiest questions of faith, and giving brilliant "dramatic expression to various types of belief, half-belief, and non-belief," he now appears content merely to tease *la condition humaine*. Before I attempt to account for the reasons behind the change and decline, let me turn to the penultimate novel.

II

The characters, plot, and themes of *The Comedians*[3] appear to be much as before, but actually they are accompanied by a change of direction, different insights, an altered tone, and, for Greene, a novel point of view.

Start with the characters. Brown, the narrator of the novel, is a homeless Englishman, short on involvement and trust, reminiscent of two of his rootless countrymen — Querry, a spiritually burnt-out case, and Fowler, the quiet American's nemesis — but he achieves a relatively more successful commitment in the end than either of them. Smith, a United States presidential candidate, has a sense of mission that recalls Pyle, the quiet American, but Smith has more heart and less destructive innocence.

[3]Half of this section devoted to *The Comedians*, with however a different conclusion, first appeared in *Renascence*, Summer 1966, pp. 219-221.

Jones, a seedy English adventurer, with a strong sense of pity, calls to mind Scobie, whose willingness to be a sacrificial victim never quite pierces to the heart of the matter, but Jones' death is more heroic. Martha, Brown's mistress, is pathetic and impulsive, like Helen, Scobie's mistress, but Martha has more nerve. Martha's husband, a Latin-American ambassador, is a complaisant cuckold, similar to Miles, but one who recovers his wife, unlike Miles, whose wife audaciously conducts an affair to the end. Doctor Magiot, the heroic Haitian physician and Brown's confidant, is another Doctor Colin, Querry's confidant, but Magiot is more robust in political faith.

Analyze the relationships among the characters. The antagonists are no longer rigidly divided into two categories, the religious sinner or the secular saint, with the paradox stretched to the breaking point. Brown is "a Catholic nothing," but he has no compulsive need to write his sins in upper case letters in order to dramatize his apostasy. Concasseur, the chief of the Tontons Macoute, a Gestapo-like police force, does not tranquilize his conscience by alternating bullying with bouts of abstinence and almsgiving. He does not have to; the "pleasure he felt in breaking limbs" is never accompanied by a sense of guilt. The protagonists are now loosely divided into two classes, "the toffs and the tarts," with the distinction blurred as often as not. Jones is a tart: he picks "a living here and there," keeps his "ears open and . . . eyes skinned," lives by his wits, and is frightened because he gets lost inside himself. Smith is a toff: he has "a settled job . . . a good income . . . a stake somewhere," and he possesses "reason, intelligence, character." Brown is difficult to diagnose: perhaps he is "a tart . . . pretending to be a toff." Never has Greeneland provided "comedians" in such abundance before. A comedian, in the Greene vernacular, is someone who wears an absurd mask and plays a part. The narrator is aware that the three names, Brown, Smith, and Jones, are "interchangeable like comic masks in a farce." When we first encounter them, all three are on a Dutch ship with a Greek name "driven by an authoritative practical joker towards the extreme point of comedy." The long arm of coincidence, usually so fell in its clutch, is here extended cordially. It is no more grim than the unlikely "encounter on the Atlantic between three people called Smith, Brown, and Jones."

Inspect the plot. *The Comedians,* a fictionalized version of life under Doctor Duvalier's dictatorship in Haiti, is a story of brutality and corruption, love and intrigue, expectation and disappointment. Brown is returning to "the shabby land of terror" to look after his failing hotel and to renew his affair with Martha. Smith and his wife, idealists both, are hoping to establish a vegetarian center in Haiti. Jones is bound there on some shady enterprise which, though obscure, involves the intention to misappropriate government funds.

Investigate the manner in which the plot is handled. The puerile sense of humor, prevalent in earlier novels of Greene, recurs. Condoms are pressed into service as balloons for a ship's concert. But since it is the work of a practical joker, at least the deception is appropriate. This was not always the case, earlier. Again, there is violence: the narrator and others are manhandled by the Tontons Macoute. But now, for the most part, it is less gratuitous. All the principal characters in *The Comedians* who are moved to violence are ultimately moved out of sympathy for the suffering of others. For them, violence is the expression of love. In Greene's previous first person novels, the narrator has often been deficient in empathy. Brown is no exception: he confesses to "a desire to hurt." He makes fun of Mr. and Mrs. Smith: for their vegetarianism, their teetotalism, and their utopian desire to free the Haitians "from acidity, poverty and passion." But he compensates for this by eventually admiring their casual charitableness and finally by imitating it. He begins by seeing them as comic figures; he ends by regarding them as heroic. Brown displays a maturity in American-baiting and a capacity for growth beyond the pale of his predecessors. And there are the usual phallic and anal preoccupations with semen, urine, and feces, but this time there is less scatological excess.

Examine the themes. In Greene's earlier novels, the love-affairs never ended without pain or regret, and love-making was always carried on in the midst of fear and fumbling. But Brown does not persistently link love and ruin, and at least once he is able to take a woman with ease and confidence — thanks to the reassuring presence of a sea-gull. A dreary blend of religion and adultery was the staple in previous novels. It recurs. Martha and Brown, lying "in a shallow declivity under the palms like bodies given a common burial," gravely discuss Catholicism while copulating. But on another occasion, this time in bed, Brown fornicates in an aura of religious euphoria: "I could imagine the taste of milk on her breasts and the taste of honey between her thighs and I could imagine for a moment that I was entering the promised land." In the past, desire was invariably accelerated by danger and uncomfortable circumstances. It still happens. Martha and Brown function well outdoors or in cramped positions in an automobile, but most of all they enjoy a frolic in bed. And, in the past, sadism and sex were sometimes bed partners. They still are. To disguise his lack of feeling towards Martha, on one occasion, Brown deliberately inflicts pain upon her, but, on other occasions, her loyalty and goodness coax gentleness from him. Again, there is Manicheanism — Brown flings himself "into pleasure like a suicide on to a pavement" — but only a pinch this time. Besides, there is Brown's "promised land" fantasy to serve as a corrective. Suicide is still the rage. A politician, who has fallen from grace, cuts his throat in a swimming pool, and the black lover of Brown's mother, upon hearing of her death, hangs himself in despair. But Greene no longer even tries to justify the desperate action.

In *The Quiet American,* for the first time, Greene surmounted the antihumanistic Catholic literary tradition which had circumscribed *Brighton Rock, The Power and the Glory, The Heart of the Matter,* and *The End of the Affair.* Henceforward, evil was to be less theological and subjective, more mundane and non-personal; and good was to be found, not in one, but, in many guises. What is new in *The Comedians* is not the breadth of sympathy characteristic of *The Quiet American* and *A Burnt-Out Case,* but the fictionalization of the existentialistic notion of the absurd. From novels conceived in terms of a tragic conflict between values, natural and supernatural, Greene has now moved on to a novel in which the anxieties and agonies of modern life conceived in terms of ironic black comedy loom over the human-divine tussle. The narrator, who may reflect his creator at this point, expresses the change simply: "Life was a comedy, not the tragedy for which I had been prepared."

Greene's gradual escape from the Catholic ghetto is a welcome change for many critics. Reviewing *A Burnt-Out Case,* John Hutchens writes:

> If there is a difference of tone between this book and such earlier Greene reflections on man and God as "The Heart of the Matter" and "The End of the Affair," it is in the direction of a certain humanizing warmth and away from the chilly austerity with which he has sometimes seemed to regard his characters. It gives to "A Burnt-Out Case" an appeal that one reader, at least, never felt in any of the other non-"Entertainment" works in the Greene canon.[4]

And Richard Boston, reviewing *Travels with My Aunt,* writes an impassioned plea in behalf of *The Comedians* as Greene's best novel on the grounds that he has "always found it easiest to take Greene's work most seriously when it has been least solemn." He goes on to argue "that not only are the Catholic novels . . . *not* his best but . . . actually among his worst."[5] But Robert Gorham Davis is not sure that the change is all to the good. Reviewing *A Burnt-Out Case,* he implies that the change is at the expense of a slight loss of imaginative intensity. "These conversations about pain and wholeness, self-love and selflessness, belief and disbelief show a changed and milder mood in Greene. Though this does not necessarily make

---

[4]*New York Herald Tribune,* February 17, 1961, p. 17.
[5]*New York Times Book Review,* January 25, 1970, p. 4.

it a better novel, "A Burnt-Out Case" is free from the theological arrogance, the baiting of rationalists, the melodramatic use of attempted bargains with God which gave a peculiar edge and intensity to Greene's earlier religious fiction."[6]

This is the heart of the matter: the price Greene has to pay for "humanizing warmth" and a "milder mood." It involves much more than a loss of "edge and intensity." Let us understand what it is he loses when he abandons those "melodramatic . . . bargains with God" and those flashy skirmishes between the flesh and the spirit that are the essence of the quartet bounded by *Brighton Rock* and *The End of the Affair*. He casts off a neo-Augustinian framework, a framework that enclosed his sinners and saints, in the words of Alice Mayhew, "caught between the Augustinian temptation to be made good, but not for awhile and the Augustinian hound who chases and harries."[7] Now I submit that this Augustinian overlay, continually distorted by his personal point of view, was the source of Greene's strength and that shorn of it he has become much like Samson shorn of his hair.

Underlying my analysis of *The Comedians* is the contention that Greene's view of Catholicism has gradually changed. His once devout but idiosyncratic Catholicism has dwindled into near-agnosticism.[8] To the extent he retains a sense of religion, it is one that has accomodated itself to the world. The former supercharged

---

[6]*New York Times Book Review*, February 19, 1961, p. 3.

[7]*Commonweal*, March 31, 1961, p. 19.

[8]In *A Sort of Life* (p. 168), Greene confesses: "With the approach of death I care less and less about religious truth. One hasn't long to wait for revelation or darkness."

Catholic atmosphere, characterized by a view extending no quarter to secularism, has given way to a bland Catholic atmosphere, characterized by a view extending comfort to Caesar. While Greene the man may be the better for having toned down the frenetic quality of his religious speculation, Greene the novelist is the loser. His novels beginning with *The Quiet American* — although a vestige of the old view is more pronounced in *A Burnt-Out Case* — are simply not as exciting and memorable as the intensely religious novels. Now I realize that this is tantamount to arguing that a "ghetto" point of view can sometimes produce finer art than a "melting-pot" outlook. But I believe just that: the shift to a majority point of view is no guarantee that a talented writer will improve his literary output. Worthsworth's intensely experienced paganism, for example, produced far finer poems than any that came out of his later faint-hearted commitment to Christianity.

Greene's literary creativity is strongest in his Catholicism-for-the-hereafter novels, where his religious assumptions are often pessimistic, extreme, and unorthodox. It is diminished in his Christianity-for-the-world novels, where his religious concerns are more relaxed, popular, and ecumenical. The earlier novels always present Catholicism as if it were a season in hell. Elsewhere I have written: "Pascal, in his *Pensées*, describes the wretchedness of man without God; Greene describes the wretchedness of man with God."[9] The Catholic characters in the earlier novels are, almost without exception, the greatest sinners in the cast. Some of these same characters,

---

[9] "Graham Greene: The Anatomy of a Catholic Novelist," *Catholic Book Reporter*, May 1961, p. 8.

ignorant of the implications of the Incarnation, associate the flesh with revulsion. But as Greene gradually substitutes a humanistic orientation for a theocentric one, things change. For example, the priests at the leproserie, in *A Burnt-Out Case,* are "more concerned over the problems of the electric-light plant or the quality of the brickmaking than over the pursuit of souls."

Ultimately my case rests with the characters and themes. I find "hilt" Catholics, like Pinkie, the whisky priest, Scobie, and Sarah — who "are as familiar with the significance of sin as they are with the air they breathe,"[10] are torn between the redemptive power of grace and the fatal attraction of evil, and are indelibly conditioned by intense reception of the sacraments — simply unforgettable. I find "nothing" Catholics, like Brown and Aunt Augusta, the heroine of *Travels with My Aunt* — for all their apelike reeling among the wheeling stars — easy to forget. And I find the theme of redemption by suffering, suffering freely chosen, more convincing than the theme of avoiding necessary suffering, by hectic but superficial involvement in life. Even then the change from Orphic preoccupation with the hereafter to Bacchic emphasis on the here and now would not matter much if the latter theme were embodied in characters about whom we were invited to care. "But most of these figures," says Denis Donoghue, referring to Greene's recent characters, "care so much for themselves that they do not need our concern. They are figures in a moving landscape, no more. They exist in latitude, not in depth."[11]

---

[10]*Ibid.,* p. 9.
[11]*New York Review of Books,* March 12, 1970.

Whereas whatever the reader's ideology he has to admit that we were invited to care about the hilt Catholic characters. They care so little for themselves that they do need our concern. They are soulscaped figures, limned in depth, engaged in nothing less than the drama of eternity.

In addition to the aforementioned reason for preferring the Catholic novels to the later novels there is another that will gradually emerge as I discuss the most recent of his novels.

III

Never were blood relatives less alike than Henry Pulling, the narrator of *Travels with My Aunt,*[12] and Augusta Bertram, apparently his aunt but acually, as it turns out, his mother. Henry, approaching his interior fifties, is "sunk deep in . . . middle age." This inhibited man with a colorless name leads a colorless life. Augusta, past seventy five, still behaves like a flower-child. Her black lover (this is the second straight novel in which an elderly white woman has a youthful black lover), Wordsworth, calls her "my bebi gel."

Henry, an unmarried retired bank manager perfectly content to eke out his remaining years cultivating dahlias, is pathetic. He exists without love. He has little interest in women; perhaps that is why the knack of drawing a woman's love has always eluded him. Those deceased who live on in the memory of loved ones are more alive

[12]The part of this section devoted to *Travels with My Aunt* first appeared, with a slightly different emphasis, in *America,* April 4, 1970, p. 373.

than he is. He envies the late Curran, much talked about as one of the two great loves of Augusta's life. Henry is loyal to establishments, not people. Security and the simple life are what he values above all: everything must be "clean and arranged and safe." He resists change. He dislikes the unexpected; it disrupts his "very regular life." He longs to regress to the Victorian world, where he feels more at home. Typically his favorite literature is Victorian poetry and fiction. And he reveals "a weakness for funerals. People are generally seen at their best on these occasions, serious and sober, and optimistic on the subject of personal immortality."

If Henry is one of the life-deniers, Augusta is presented as "one of the life-givers." Her knowledge of human experience is supposed to be as full as his is empty. She cultivates a streak of anarchy, vulgarity, devilry, and risk-taking. A courtesan with a high regard for love, she chooses adventurous and imaginative lovers, men with the potential to keep her amused. She extols incessant traveling as a way of prolonging the good life and expresses a desire to die on her travels. The author would have it that she defeats death by living all the way up; that she has discovered the secret of lasting youth. Above all, she is a delightful companion who tells spellbinding stories by the hour.

Under the belated tutelage of this mother — whom he has been ignorant of, separated from, and has considered only as his aunt for fifty years — Henry gradually and painfully learns how to crawl into life, so that by the end of the novel he can say that he feels "oddly elated to be alive."

Travels with My Aunt represents a departure from Graham Greene's usual fiction. The reason in part is the self-parody: here Greene jokes about all the things he used to brood about — cremation, crime, death, religion, sex, and sin. In part, it is the technique: for this "novel" is really a protracted character sketch. Wherever Henry and Augusta travel, the locale inspires one of Augusta's exotic stories. Brighton, for instance, affords her the opportunity to recount "the history of the dog's church"; Paris, the affair with Monsieur Dambreuse, "the gallant lover who had kept two mistresses in the same hotel" at the same time; the Orient Express to Istanbul, Mr. Visconti's escape from the Allied troops, dressed up as a monsignor, and his Vatican swindle; Boulogne, the unsuccessful attempt of William Curlew to cuckold himself.

The site, the actual events that take place there, the characters met — all shrink before Augusta's powers as a raconteur, until finally one begins to wonder if everything else and everyone else are not put there simply as an excuse for her to exercise those powers. If it were not for the unfaltering Greene style, coaxing far-fetched plot details and often silly dialogue to click into place like the tumblers in a lock, this would be little more than an extended visit to "My Most Unforgettable Character," courtesy of the *Reader's Digest*. As it is, Greene's "unforgettable character" actually is almost as easily forgotten as the *Reader's Digest* species. For Augusta pays the price of appearing in a waxworks story: she remains an unconvincing life-force figure. It was not always thus in Greene's fiction. One reason why Pinkie, for instance, is a convincing death-force figure is that he is not superior to the story in which he occupies the center of the stage.

Travels with My Aunt highlights the additional reason for the gradual change and decline in Greene's work. It has to do with the nature of his gallows humor. Parody and especially self-parody which have been lurking in Greene's work, as far back as *Loser Takes All,* come out of the shadows with the appearance of *Travels with My Aunt.* Now a sense of humor is something that was lacking in Greene's fiction prior to *Loser Takes All,* and other things being equal, touches of humor should have made for Greener pastures. But, as we have seen, other things did not remain equal: the theme changed in part to accomodate the humor, and the characters slumped. The Greener pastures never materialized because of a disastrous change of mentors, around 1955. At this time, the Evelyn Waugh mystique began gradually to gain a hold over him; as this hold tightened, the collective Conrad-James-Mauriac hold loosened.

Ever since Greene pseudonymously won a prize in a *New Statesman* competition for parodying himself, he has been hooked on self-parody: a frank, deliberate mocking of a life-attitude which permeated the author's books through *The End of the Affair.* The addiction peaks in *Travels with My Aunt,* a novel, in the words of Christopher Lehmann-Haupt, "that is the flip side of everything dark and threatening that has ever brooded in Graham Greene's fiction." And the reviewer cites chapter and verse, when he adds:

And Henry and Augusta travel together—to Brighton Beach, to Istanbul on the Orient Express, to South America, to all the places that Graham Greene has been writing about these many years.

It's Graham Greene joking about all the things he used to brood about — religion, sex, crime, Interpol. It's Graham Greene indulging in a considerable amount of forced whimsey, too. But the touch is still so smooth and fluid that . . . only a spoilsport would say that "Travels with My Aunt" is wasted effort; that reading it is like watching Ted Williams apply the grace of his swing to the mere beating of a rug.[13]

Call me a "spoilsport": long before the end of the novel, the parody has run out of steam.

Evelyn Waugh is the acknowledged master of sustained parody, in our time. With triumphantly ingenious and inventive skill, he prolongs a constantly rising tempo of absurdities and pseudo-logical plausibility. But Greene cannot sustain these elements, and so he was ill-advised to change mentors. Perhaps he was motivated to imitate Waugh by Waugh's earlier decision to imitate him. *Brideshead Revisited* (1946) is Waugh's unsuccessful attempt at a serious Catholic novel. The measure of its inferiority to *Decline and Fall* is as considerable as the inferiority of *Travels with My Aunt* to *The Power and the Glory*. There is a likely moral here: shoemaker stick to thy last!

[13]*New York Times*, January 19, 1970.

Undoubtedly, after a series of successes in one area, the temptation to turn to a different genre is strong in some writers, and when the switch is successful the writer deserves applause. But when the change is deleterious, the novelist should be discouraged, for his own good, from continuing in the new vein. Prudent self-criticism and not taking one's self too seriously are virtues, of course, but Greene does not stop there. He denies the very works on which his reputation rests. It is one thing when he satirizes his critics, as he does in "A Visit to Morin" and *The End of the Affair*. It is another when he satirizes himself, as he does in *Travels with My Aunt*. When Henry and his aunt go to Brighton, for example, he learns of an episode in her past when she ran a church for dogs with "the Rev. Curran" (Rev. for Revered, not Reverend). She tells him: "Curran wanted to start the churching of bitches after the puppies came, but I said that was going too far — even the Church of England has abandoned churching." The scene of Pinkie's spiritual torment is thus farcically cut down to the question of whether or not dogs have souls. This is wantonly unhealthy: a most apprehensive novelist castrating himself so as to disarm hostile critics. This remarkable potential for self-destruction is an important issue, since it also raises the question of Greene's integrity.

Appendix
The Role of Dreams in Greene's Fiction

IN *Journey Without Maps*, Greene tells us that his earliest dreams did not belong to the Christian imagination. The beings who peopled those faraway dreams were neither good nor evil: they simply controlled power. "It is the earliest dream that I can remember . . . this dream of something outside that has got to come in. . . . This is simply power, a force exerted on a door, an influence that drifted after me upstairs and pressed against windows." Many years passed before his dreams acquired an overlay of evil. "It was only many years later that Evil came into my dreams: the man with gold teeth and rubber surgical gloves; the old woman with ringworm; the man with his throat cut dragging himself across the carpet to the bed."

The first dream that Greene recounts in his first novel, *The Man Within*, is like his own earliest dream. Andrews dreams of Carlyon, a man indifferent to good or evil, a man whose attitude towards experience is amoral. Then only a few hours later Andrews dreams that men are imputing courage to his father, a virtue that his deceased father really did not possess but only seemed to in the eyes of his cutthroat associates. Moral issues are fleet intruders into Andrews' dreams. Fiction moves at a faster pace than fact: the advent of evil is greatly accelerated in the fictional dream.

As Kenneth Allott points out: "This is the first example of Greene's use of dreams to convey information and deepen a sense of character. His course of psycho-analytic treatment mentioned in 'The Revolver in the Corner Cupboard' probably has something to do with his fondness for a device used very frequently; most boldly, perhaps, in Raven's dreams in *This Gun for Hire* and Arthur Rowe's in *The Ministry of Fear*."[1] An examination of Raven's two dreams, in the railway shed where he sleeps in the course of his flight from the police, bears out Allott's contention.

Falling asleep from exhaustion, Raven first dreams that "the old minister was coming towards him, saying, 'Shoot me. Shoot me in the eyes,' and Raven was a child with a catapult in his hands. He wept and wouldn't shoot, and the old minister said, 'Shoot, dear child. We'll go home together. Shoot.'"

This dream may well be interpreted in the light of Raven's notion, alluded to more than once, that Christ had consented to His own death. The minister is then a Christ figure who not only dies willingly ("Shoot, dear child. We'll go home together. Shoot") but dies for others as well. He pleads for the death meted out to his secretary ("Shoot me in the eyes").

Later, when Raven falls asleep again:

He dreamed that he was building a great bonfire on Guy Fawkes Day. He threw in everything he could find: a saw-edged knife, a lot of racing cards, the leg of a table. It burned warmly, deeply, beautifully. A lot of fireworks were going off all round him, and again the old war minister appeared on the other side of the fire. He said, "It's a good fire," stepping into it himself. Raven ran to the fire to pull him out, but the old man said, "Let me be. It's warm here," and then he sagged like a Guy Fawkes in the flames.

[1] Allott, *op. cit.*, p. 57.

The second dream retains the association of the minister with Christ but adds new associations connected with death. Since the minister, like Guy Fawkes, was a conspirator who met a violent end, it is fitting that Raven should merge the two men in his dream. Other memories, more personal and unpleasant, provide fuel for the flames: the kitchen knife refers to his mother's suicide; the table-leg to the table on which he saw her bleed; the racing cards to his membership in a razor-wielding race track gang.

Both dreams attest to Raven's sense of guilt, pity, and regret ("He wept and wouldn't shoot." "Raven ran to the fire to pull him out"). If we allow for the possibility that the minister may also be Raven's double, then both dreams constitute an expression of a death wish on Raven's part (" 'Shoot me.' " " 'Let me be. It's warm here,' and then he sagged like a Guy Fawkes in the flames").

Rowe's dreams, as feverish as Raven's, likewise tighten the screw of nightmare omnipresent in Greene's thrillers. Two dreams, in an underground shelter during a London air raid, in which a rat appears illustrate how Rowe's unconscious mind wanders "freely in that strange world where the past and future leave equal traces, and the geography may belong to twenty years ago or to next year."

In the first dream, when Rowe recalls how as a child, moved by pity, he bludgeoned a rat with a broken back to death, the geography belongs to the remote past. But since this boyhood peccadillo foreboded the mercy killing of his wife, before the book opens, the geography belongs also to the proximate past. The second dream takes a prophetic turn, however, when a policeman urges "him remorselessly towards a urinal where a rat bled to death in the slate trough.. .and ... where even the ground whined when he pressed it as if it had learned the trick of suffering." This dream predates reality: the villain Hilfe subsequently kills himself in a lavatory, while "the floor of the urinal whined under his feet" during a bombing raid; at the same time, Rowe, a witness to the event, "thought of a dead rat and a policeman."

In the thrillers, where violence calls the tune, Greene's dreamers do one of two things: either they escape reality, like Professor D. in *The Confidential Agent*, or they exaggerate it, like chorus girl Coral Musker in *Orient Express*. "Only in sleep," Greene reports on the former, "did he evade violence; his dreams were almost invariably made up of peaceful images from the past. Compensation? Wish-fulfillment? He was no longer interested in his own psychology. He dreamed of lecture rooms, his wife, sometimes of food and wine, very often of flowers." The latter dreams that "she danced and danced and danced in the glare of the spot-light, and the producer struck at her bare legs with a cane, telling her she was no good, that she was a month late, that she'd broken her contract. And all the time she danced and danced and danced, taking no notice of him while he beat at her legs with the cane."

The two worlds of peace and violence are also reflected in the dreams of the characters in the Catholic novels. The night the Mexican priest, during his pursuit, spends in a hot and crowded cell, he has a nightmare in which "his child lay beside him bleeding to death," in front of a doctor's house. "He banged on the door and shouted, 'Even if I can't think of the right word, haven't you a heart?' The child was dying and looked up at him with middle-aged, complacent wisdom. She said, 'You animal,' and he woke again crying." After his capture, the night before he is to be executed, he dreams he is going towards peace.

Major Scobie, too, has pleasant and unpleasant dreams, subject to this difference: since Scobie loses himself—whereas the Priest finds himself—his dreams become progressively less carefree, less comforting. In the first book of *The Heart of the Matter*, for instance, Scobie dreams of "walking through a wide cool meadow with Ali at his heels: there was nobody else anywhere in his dream, and Ali never spoke. Birds went by far overhead, and once when he sat down the grass was parted by a small green snake which passed onto his hand and up his arm without fear and before it slid down into the grass again touched his cheek with a cold friendly remote tongue." His subsequent dreams in Book One, however, are more disquieting, and the dream he has in Book Three is most disquieting.

When the use that Greene makes of dreams in the entertainments is compared with the use he makes of dreams in the Catholic novels, the following differences become apparent. While characters in the one genre dream with about the same degree of frequency as characters in the other genre (usually two to four dreams per hero) and while the purpose of the dreams is the same (to reveal the character's innermost nature), the dreams in the novels are frequently novel (whereas the dreams in the entertainments are rarely entertaining) and subtle, as well as less obtrusive and less logical.

The two following dreams, comparably long, typify the differences.

Myatt, in *Orient Express*, having given his pullman compartment to Coral, sleeps uneasily in the corridor outside:

The rush of the loosed steam and the draught on his cheek contributed to his dream. The corridor became the long straight Spaniards Road with the heath on either side. He was being driven slowly by Isaacs in his Bentley, and they watched the girls' faces as they walked in pairs along the lamp-lit eastern side, shopgirls offering themselves dangerously for a drink at the inn, a fast ride, and the fun of the thing. . . . Isaacs drew up the Bentley under a lamp and they let the anonymous young beautiful animal faces stream by. Isaacs wanted someone fair and plump and Myatt someone thin and dark, but it was not easy to pick and choose, for all along the eastern side were lined the cars of their competitors, girls leaning across the open doors laughing and smoking. . . . Myatt was irritated by Isaac's uncompromising taste; it was cold in the Bentley with a draught on the cheek, and presently when he saw Coral Musker walking by, he jumped from the car and offered her a cigarette and after that a drink and after that a ride. . . .

Just before the end, the Priest, in *The Power and the Glory*, has a curious dream:

He dreamed he was sitting at a café table in front of the high altar of the cathedral. About six dishes were spread before him, and he was eating hungrily. There was a smell of incense and an odd sense of elation. The dishes . . . did not taste of much, but he had a sense that when he had finished them, he would have the best dish of all. A priest passed to and fro before the altar saying Mass, but he took no notice: the service no longer seemed to concern him. At last the six plates were empty; someone out of sight rang the sanctus bell, and the serving priest knelt before he raised the Host. But *he* sat on, just waiting, paying no attention to the God over the altar, as though that were a God for other people and not for him. Then the glass by his plate began to fill with wine, and looking up he saw that the child from the banana station was serving him. She said, "I got it from my father's room.". . .

Myatt's conscious mind rules his dream too much, and Greene himself relies excessively on this dream to convey to the reader knowledge of Myatt's sexual habits. By contrast, in the Priest's case the dream rules the dreamer: the thread of logic is broken. Myatt's dreams establish his character; the

Priest's dreams intensify his already established character. Even when dreams are used in the entertainments to heighten the significance of something already known to the reader, as we saw in the analysis of Raven's dreams, the incongruity and unpredictability necessary to make a dream totally convincing are never present to as great a degree as they are in the dreams that appear in the novels. Thus, Greene's presentation of the dream device is more skillful in the later novels.

Bibliography

Only books by Graham Greene are listed. The editions given are those cited in the text and in the footnotes. The copyright date is noted within brackets only when different from the publication date. For a nearly complete list of works *on* Greene see J. Don Vann's *Graham Greene: A Checklist of Criticism* (Kent State University Press, 1970).

A Burnt-Out Case. New York: Viking, 1961.

Another Mexico. New York: Viking, 1939. British title *The Lawless Roads.*

Brighton Rock. New York: Viking, 1938.

Carving a Statue. London: Bodley Head, 1964.

The Comedians. New York: Viking, 1966.

The Complaisant Lover. London: Heinemann, 1959.

The End of the Affair. New York: Viking, 1951.

The Heart of the Matter. New York: Viking, 1948.

In Search of a Character. New York: Viking, 1962.

It's a Battlefield. London: Heinemann, 1948 [1934].

Journey Without Maps. London: Heinemann, 1950 [1936].

The Living Room. New York: Viking, 1954.

Loser Takes All. New York: Viking, 1957 [1955].

The Lost Childhood and Other Essays. New York: Viking, 1952 [1951]. When this was reprinted in 1969, the title was changed to *Collected Essays.*

The Man Within. New York: Viking, 1947 [1929].

May We Borrow Your Husband? New York: Viking, 1967.

Nineteen Stories. New York: Viking, 1949 [1947]. When this was reprinted, with two additional stories, in 1955, the title was changed to *Twenty-One Stories*.

Orient Express. New York: Doubleday, 1933 [1932]. British title *Stamboul Train*.

Our Man in Havana. New York: Viking, 1958.

The Old School, Essays by Divers Hands. Edited and with an introduction and essay, "The Last Word." London: Jonathan Cape, 1934.

The Potting Shed. New York: Viking, 1957.

The Power and the Glory. New York: Viking, 1946 [1940]. Formerly entitled *The Labyrinthine Ways*.

The Quiet American. New York: Viking, 1956.

A Sense of Reality. New York: Viking, 1963.

The Shipwrecked. New York: Viking, 1953 [1935]. British title *England Made Me*.

A Sort of Life. New York: Simon and Schuster, 1971.

The Third Man. New York: Viking, 1950.

Three by Graham Greene. New York: Viking, 1952. Incl.:

    This Gun for Hire. New York: Viking, 1936. British title *A Gun for Sale*.

    The Confidential Agent. New York: Viking, 1939.

    The Ministry of Fear. New York: Viking, 1943.

Travels with My Aunt. New York: Viking, 1970.

INDEX